COLD AGAINST DISEASE

THE
WONDERS
OF COLD

LUCY KAVALER

COLD AGAINST DISEASE

The John Day Company • New York

Published in Canada by Fitzhenry & Whiteside Limited, Toronto.

Library of Congress Catalogue Card Number: 69–10810
Printed in the United States of America
Designed by The Etheredges
ISBN 0-381-99773-1

10 9 8 7 6 5 4 3 2

For my mother

HELEN VISHNIAC ESTRIN

In loving memory

CONTENTS

COLD AGAINST DISEASE

1. COLD, BEARER OF LIFE AND DEATH

The snow fell steadily from leaden skies, melting just enough upon reaching the ground to form a soggy, muddy slush. It was the bitter winter of 1784 and a troop of Scottish soldiers on horseback was stumbling through the muck on its way from Glasgow to the Highlands. The horses' hooves kept slipping, almost throwing the riders time and again. Behind the horsemen straggled an even more pathetic group made up of the wives and children accompanying the soldiers to the new posting. They huddled close together sharing body warmth as the wind whistled through the barren branches of the trees and cut through their threadbare clothing. Those who were too small to walk

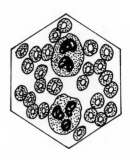

were carried in baskets fastened to the saddles of their fathers' horses. Almost naked and covered with only the thinnest of blankets, they whimpered from the cold.

The men and women seldom complained about the cold. They lived in terror of something far worse—smallpox. At that time this scourge had not yet been conquered, and an epidemic was raging. Each day the number of those stricken rose. Many of the children fell victim to the disease. But a surprising thing happened: Most had only a mild form of the illness and recovered.

No one understood how this could be, and the parents for the most part agreed that there must have been a mistake and that the children had not really been sick with the pox. Eventually a medical report was written about the events of the journey, but doctors were no more ready than uneducated people to accept the reason given for the comparatively gentle course taken by the illness. The truth was so strange that even today it is hard to believe that the children were saved by cold. The chill air and biting wind had lowered body temperatures. A cold body functions more slowly than a warm one, and so is less affected by disease processes. In this condition, then, the children were better able to withstand the ravages of smallpox than their fathers who were protected from the cold by the army uniforms.

This explanation was not accepted, because no one could believe cold to be of value. To this day, most people think cold is harmful. They associate it with illness and with death. And that is true; cold does bring death every year.

The winter of 1967 was the coldest in 50 years in the small country of Mongolia that lies between China and the USSR. The temperature on the grassy steppes where the livestock graze fell to −50° and then to −60° Fahrenheit. By the time spring came, two million animals were dead. The following winter was no milder and another two million head were lost. Cold thus did great harm to the economy of this underdeveloped nation struggling to advance and raise its standard of living.

In the industrialized United States, too, animals are overcome by cold every year. Nearly 30,000 deer perished in Wisconsin in the course of a particularly frigid winter.

COLD, BEARER OF LIFE AND DEATH

A middle-aged Tennessee woman went into her backyard during a cold snap. She stumbled and fell and was too stunned to get up at once. The following morning her next-door neighbor looked over the fence and was shocked to see her frozen corpse. In Europe on a December day a year or so ago, a body was found lying in the snow in the mountains near Zurich, Switzerland. Once it had been identified as that of a well-known physician, rumors spread all over Zurich that murder had been done. This very man a short time before had been called in to examine the body of a famous person who had met a mysterious death. Perhaps, went the speculation, the doctor had concealed the evidence of murder and had been killed in his turn to guarantee his silence. An autopsy revealed no hint of foul play. The professor had apparently gone out for a walk, been overcome by the cold, and had frozen to death. Cold alone had been to blame.

Even when it does not kill, cold can injure. A single hospital in Denver, Colorado, in an average year admits seven people with frostbitten toes and fingers. Frostbite has been a particular problem in military operations in cold climates. Four centuries before the birth of Christ, the Greek general and historian, Xenophon, led an army in retreat across the Carduchian Mountains. The soldiers suffered from the piercing winds and biting cold. "Toes dropped off from frostbite," Xenophon wrote in his account of the campaign. Since then ways of guarding against frostbite have been found, and even at McMurdo Sound, the main United States station in Antarctica, there are only three cases in a typical winter.

Cold can also make a number of heart or circulatory conditions

15

much worse. Prisoners in Siberian labor camps have been found to suffer from high blood pressure, particularly on bitter days.

Most people hate cold, and with reason. The sensation of shivering in the wind is miserable; the nose grows red and raw, the feet numb, the hands chapped and ugly. Cold has an effect on the emotions as well as the body. Fits of depression can seize usually cheerful individuals in intensely frigid weather, while others become exceedingly irritable.

"A gloomy melancholy air lowered on the brows of our shipmates, and a dreadful silence reigned among us . . . the hour of dinner was hateful," wrote a sailor traveling through icy Antarctic waters in the eighteenth century.

Yet this very same cold that can bring misery and death can also cure in ways that seem mysterious. In 1965, for example, a 35-year-old woman lay dying. Born with a malformed heart, every moment of her life had been a struggle. She had driven herself to go to school, to marry, and to adopt a baby girl. Still, willpower was not enough and at last it seemed that her struggle was approaching its end. Too weak to go outside, she lay in her room, her face pale and bluish as a result of the poor circulation of the blood. She was saved in the end by an operation she could not have survived at a normal body temperature. Instead, she was chilled to 68°F. A month after the surgery she went home to her husband and child. A year later she was learning to play golf.

A 10-year-old child with an unusual blood type was badly injured in an accident. He could not use any of the types available in the local blood bank. A vial of frozen blood that matched his was flown from a distant medical center.

An aged woman nearly blind had her sight restored when a cataract was frozen off her eye. A brain tumor that no surgeon of the past, however skillful, could have reached, in modern times has been destroyed by cold. Childless couples have had babies fathered by frozen sperm.

Gradually our attitude toward cold is changing. After thousands of years in which man considered cold to be an enemy, he is coming to see it as an ally in his battle against disease. Then, too, researchers are correcting many misconceptions about cold that make it seem worse than it is.

Practically everybody accepts it as fact that cold weather brings on the common cold. Now a group of doctors at Baylor University College of Medicine, Houston, Texas, have shown that cold has in this case been blamed unjustly. Volunteers, wearing only light cotton shorts, were injected with a cold virus and put into a room cooled to 40°F. By the time they came out, they were chilled, shivering, and miserable. Everyone expected them to have colds by morning. The expected failed to happen. A few of them did catch cold, but so did some of a second group of volunteers who had stayed warm to provide a basis for comparison.

Everyone "knows" that cold, wet feet today mean a scratchy throat and clogged nose tomorrow. But this belief, too, cannot stand up to scientific study. The obliging group of Baylor volunteers got wet as well as cold and again no more colds resulted than among the people who kept their socks dry. Although many newspapers reported this, mothers have not become more lenient about letting children go out in the rain without their rubbers.

COLD AGAINST DISEASE

But what about the fact that there really are many more colds in winter than in summer? The reason is that people are indoors more in the cold weather. They stay close together and exchange cold viruses. The astronauts in the 1968 mission of Apollo 7 were neither chilled nor wet, but they were very close together in the cramped capsule. Capt. Walter M. Schirra, Jr., had a cold and quickly passed it on to his crew members, Maj. Donn F. Eisele and Walter R. Cunningham.

It is easier to say what cold can and cannot do than it is to answer the question, what is cold? Many people define cold as any temperature below 32°F, the freezing point of water. But this is too limited a definition; it is not even always true for water. The freezing point varies somewhat, depending on the salt content of water and the atmospheric pressure. In addition, it is hard to apply this definition to living things, despite their large water content. We feel cold at temperatures much warmer than 32°F.

A far better definition describes cold in terms of activity: Cold is the slowing of the movements of the molecules that make up all matter. As the temperature drops, they move more and more sluggishly. When it reaches −459.69°F, known as absolute zero, all activity stops. Such cold is characteristic of the universe. The stars themselves are hot, but the vast spaces between are three degrees above absolute zero.

It might seem then that this definition has nothing to do with life; yet these words can be applied to everything that lives. Activity is a characteristic of life. Each living cell takes in nourishment in order to build protoplasm and obtain energy and then goes on to destroy matter and to eliminate the waste. This entire process is known as metabolism and, as in the case of the children with smallpox, it is dependent upon temperature. The colder the living cell, the slower its activity. Low temperature, thus, is reflected in a low metabolic rate and high temperature in a high one.

How cold is cold? That depends on the organism and its normal temperature range. A cold-blooded Antarctic fish can swim vigorously in an ocean so frigid that it has brought the temperature of its body fluids to below the customary freezing point of water. On the other hand, the tropical sloth shivers when the temperature of the night air is a balmy 80°F.

2. REPRODUCTION BY WAY OF THE FREEZER

At this very moment somewhere in America a calf is being born. The mother cow has never been close to the bull who is the father. She has never watched him come charging across the fields to her, nor heard him bellow with joy. In fact, the bull has been dead for three years.

How then could he beget a calf? This seeming impossibility became possible because of cold. The sperm, or male reproductive cells, were taken from the bull when he was in his prime, and were frozen and stored. As he was a particularly magnificent beast, healthy and strong, his sperm was used again and again. Small quantities were thawed from time to time and injected into cows. Under normal conditions of

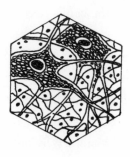

courtship, the bull may select one cow and stay with her for life; certain species of cattle are most faithful to their mates. A bull, therefore, may father the offspring of just one cow, passing his valuable traits to only a few calves. The frozen sperm from that very same bull can be used to beget not one, 10, 20, or even 100 calves, but literally several thousands.

Animal breeding has been revolutionized by the use of frozen sperm. In any given year, four million or more calves are born in the United States alone to dairy cows who have been made pregnant by frozen semen.

COLD AGAINST DISEASE

But while this agricultural use is new, efforts to freeze sperm began a long time ago. In 1776, Lazzaro Spallanzani, Italian biologist and university professor, took the reproductive cells from frogs, horses, and men, placing them out of doors on a bitter cold, snowy winter's day. After half an hour he took these samples, which looked frozen stiff, back inside. As soon as he rewarmed them, however, the sperm revived and began to move again.

No one paid very much attention to Spallanzani's account of his experiments. Scientists of his own and the following generations dismissed him with the comment that the cold had not been severe enough to freeze the sperm completely in the first place.

Ninety years were to pass before biologist P. Mantegazza made another attempt. He froze human sperm to 5°F and then brought it back to active life. Mantegazza was a man of vision: Why not, he said, set up a frozen sperm bank? Any man who wished to guarantee himself an unbroken line of descendants would arrange to have some of his sperm frozen and stored. Then if he died young on the battlefield, or as a result of illness, this would not be the end of his line. Long after his death, he could still become a father. If that idea seems shocking today, one can imagine how it appeared to people in Mantegazza's day. They viewed him as more an idle dreamer than a practical scientist.

Mantegazza had not limited himself to the human race. He suggested that the semen of superior animals be frozen and then shipped from farm to farm to be used to better the breeds of cattle, horses, and pigs.

REPRODUCTION BY WAY OF THE FREEZER

It was his aim then in 1866 to modernize artificial insemination, a method used by animal breeders for centuries. Seven hundred years ago, the Arabs injected sperm taken from prize stallions into as many mares as possible. At that time refrigeration was most primitive and there was no good way of preserving the semen. The mares, therefore, had to be ready and waiting while the sperm was being taken. Cold could change all that, said Mantegazza. But no one else saw what he did—not then, nor for decades afterward.

Mantegazza's reports met the same fate as Spallanzani's and lay yellowing and unread as the years went by. Then in 1938, long after Spallanzani and Mantegazza were dead, scientist F. Jahnel began to do research on syphilis, a venereal disease spread by sexual intercourse. In order to study the condition of the male reproductive cells more closely, he placed them in test tubes and plunged these into baths of liquid gases, bringing the temperature down far below zero. Some were held for as long as 40 days at a temperature of $-110°F$; others were frozen to $-320°F$. When Jahnel thawed the test tubes, he saw the sperm within begin to move again.

After Jahnel's report was published, scientists all over the world suddenly saw the possibilities of freezing living cells and a vast amount of research got underway. Biologists worked on sperm, blood, skin, tumor tissue, bone marrow, and a large number of other human and animal cells.

But as the number and types of cells frozen increased, it became clear that the problems of freezing had not been solved entirely. Many

25

cells died and others were injured. Some of the sperm cells seemed to revive, but later failed to fertilize the female egg.

Why did this happen? And to get to the basic questions, how does cold produce injury? How does cold kill? These questions seem almost too easy, but even today scientists are not altogether certain that they know the answers. It appears most likely that death or damage results from changes in the water that makes up a large portion of every living cell. When this water freezes, the salts that were dissolved in it are left; they become so highly concentrated that they can injure the cell. In addition, the water must hold the protein molecules essential to life in a proper pattern within the cell. Should the water freeze into ice crystals, the pattern may collapse.

Cellular death does not come rapidly or easily. Cells are far less fragile than they seem. Take out a third, even half, of the water within and most animal cells will survive—provided that ice crystals do not form inside the cell. Where else could the crystals go? Cells are packed together in such a way that some space lies between them. When the temperature is brought down slowly, the water that is inside the cell passes out of it very gradually and the ice crystals form in the outer space. If the freezing is too fast, however, there is no time for the water to do this and the ice crystals form within the cell. By now scientists know just how rapidly to freeze cells in order to prevent the ice crystals from forming in the wrong place: The temperature must be dropped at a rate of 1.8 degrees per minute. This works so well that it is often described as "the magical formula for success."

REPRODUCTION BY WAY OF THE FREEZER

Timing alone will not save a cell, unless water molecules are held in place during the entire freezing process. A substance able to do that was discovered in 1949 by a woman scientist, Dr. Audrey Smith, and two associates at the National Institute for Medical Research in London. Like many major scientific findings, this one had actually been made earlier, but the reports had been completely ignored. The discovery was almost too simple to be believed: Dr. Smith took a common cheap chemical, glycerol, and added it to bull semen just before freezing. Far more sperm cells survived than ever had before.

Later, a second substance that can also protect cells during the freezing process was discovered in a chemical by-product of wood pulp manufacture. Its scientific name is dimethyl sulfoxide and it is generally known as DMSO.

If the frozen cells are to be stored for long, not only glycerol or DMSO, but also incredibly low temperatures are needed. The means to achieve them lies in the air around us. During the eighteenth century, French chemist Antoine Lavoisier suggested that the air could be made liquid if only it were cooled enough. He since has been proved right. All the gases that make up our atmosphere have been chilled in the laboratory to temperatures that do not occur naturally on our planet and in the process, they have condensed. In order to move from the gaseous to the liquid state, oxygen must be cooled to −297.33°F, neon to −410.8°F, and hydrogen to −432.2°F. Helium is the coldest of all; it remains a gas until the temperature drops to −452°F.

A new technology has evolved, based on the use of these gases. It has been named cryogenics after the Greek word "kryos" meaning cold. Liquid gases make possible the manufacture of incredibly powerful magnets and atom smashers as well as exceedingly small computers. The thrust of liquid hydrogen and liquid oxygen lifts rockets off the ground and sends spacecraft on journeys to the moon and beyond. The application of cryogenic gases to living things is a part of the new scientific field of cryobiology.

With these gases, living cells have been taken to lower and ever lower temperatures. Cells were brought to the very edge of life and frozen in liquid helium to within seven degrees of absolute zero ($-459.69°F$). All life processes come to a complete halt. Then the cells were rewarmed and they returned to life again. They resumed functioning as if not an instant had passed since they were plunged into the liquid gas.

"Suspended animation in isolated cells and tissues is in fact a reality," Dr. Harold T. Meryman, Assistant Research Director of the Blood Program of the American National Red Cross, told a New York Academy of Sciences conference a few years ago. "Man has altered the time dimension of his existence, since, for the red cell, the sperm . . . suspended at low temperature time does in fact stand still."

Just how long can time stand still for the cell? Research studies contradict one another. Human sperm stored for 4 years has produced healthy offspring. Red blood preserved by cold for 10 years has been analyzed and found to be in perfect condition for transfusions. On the other hand, a laboratory technician tested other blood cells kept for only 2 years and observed some slight damage.

REPRODUCTION BY WAY OF THE FREEZER

From a practical viewpoint, though, even if any changes do occur, they are too minor to make any significant differences. Freezing works so well that it has improved our health and that of animals.

Successful preservation of sperm and other living matter does not require the extreme cold that liquid helium can provide. Cells go into suspended animation long before a temperature approaching the absolute zero point is reached. Nitrogen, which becomes liquid at $-320°F$ and remains in that state until chilled below $-346°F$, has been selected as the most efficient gas for general use.

To be sure, not all cells survive even now with liquid nitrogen, glycerol, and DMSO. Nearly a third of human sperm cells die during the freezing process. Bull semen is less able to endure cold and about 45 per cent is lost. Even so, enough is left to make the task worthwhile.

Agricultural experts urge that frozen sperm of a variety of animals be sent to underdeveloped countries where centuries of near-starvation have weakened the livestock. Even when agricultural improvement programs are started by the local governments it takes decades to improve the breeds. Frozen sperm of high-quality stock can be shipped in containers cooled with liquid nitrogen. The very first animals to be born gain from the heritage of strength and health provided by the absent father whose sperm was used. Both bull and goat semen endure freezing well. In some regions goats are the more common of the two, with goat milk and meat used in place of cow milk and beef.

Frozen sperm might produce an entire generation of horses each capable of winning the Kentucky Derby. With all horses equal, however, there would be no point in running the Derby at all. The Thor-

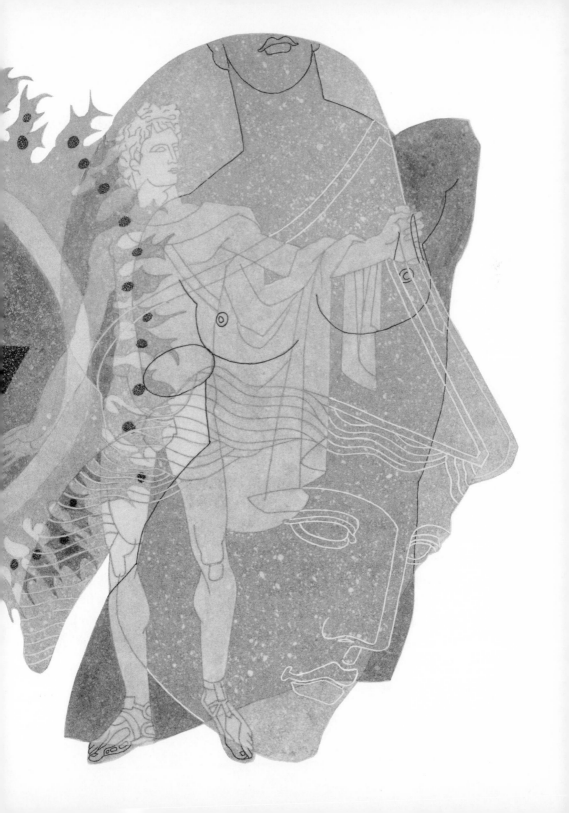

oughbred Racing Association, therefore, will not permit such a use of semen. In areas where horses are bred for farm work, rather than racing, artificial insemination could be most useful.

For all the successes with frozen sperm, breeders have their failures, too. In some cases they do not know when to inseminate the animal. Only the male pig is certain when a female pig is in heat and ready to ovulate. The most experienced farmer may miss the moment altogether. Even if he guesses right, he will not necessarily be pleased with the results since pig sperm does not freeze very well.

Researchers have not yet solved the problem of inseminating hens successfully. Rooster semen has been frozen and injected, but the chicken embryos failed to develop normally. The glycerol used in the freezing process appears to be responsible. When the problem is solved —as laboratory workers expect it to be—the necessity of reeducating chicken farmers will remain. At this time, artificial insemination with unfrozen semen is done in an illogical way: The sperm from all the roosters on the farm is pooled. The good and the bad are mixed together. Instead, only the best of the birds should be used as breeding stock.

Although laboratory tests show that dog semen loses none of its strength when frozen, dog breeders are not encouraged to use it. The pedigreed poodle bred with frozen sperm would almost surely be disqualified from winning the dog show. There is a very strange breeding rule: Artificial insemination is allowed, but shipment of sperm is not. There seems little point in freezing the sperm if both animals must be present at breeding time.

REPRODUCTION BY WAY OF THE FREEZER

Most people believe that artificial insemination is possible for rather large animals only. Who has even given a thought to the sex life of the herring? Yet herring spermatozoa as well as that of the trout and other game fish can be frozen and later injected into the eggs laid by the female.

Frozen sperm is being used in the laboratory, as well as in the stream or on the farm. Some years ago a scientist was testing various cancer treatments on one generation of rats after the other. His work was thrown off, because the rats often gave birth to mutants, which differed from others of their species. There was no way for the scientist to compare the reactions of such a new generation of rats with those of earlier groups. Today he freezes and stores the sperm of each male. Whenever he wishes to check back to an earlier stage of his research, he defrosts a certain vial and produces a rat of the desired generation.

Of all uses for frozen sperm, none is as exciting as human artificial insemination. Mantegazza's sperm bank is moving from theory into practice and is at last receiving the support of serious thinkers.

"Here we have nothing to lose, but we and the world have everything to gain," explained the late Dr. Herman J. Muller, geneticist and Nobel Prize winner.

So far no one has gone as far as Dr. Muller or Mantegazza would have wished. Efforts have not yet been made to freeze the sperm of soldiers about to go into battle or astronauts preparing to venture into space. The reproductive cells of brilliant scientists and musicians are not being placed in a sperm bank for later withdrawal by women who would like to bear the offspring of genius. Today the sperm for freezing is taken from any healthy volunteer donor. It is used in the same way as is unfrozen sperm—for artificial insemination in cases where a couple is unable to produce a child in the usual manner.

If man is to deal with heredity successfully, he must freeze the female as well as the male cells. While chilling the male cells has been surprisingly easy, the female continue to be baffling to biologists. Egg cells or ova are easily damaged or killed by freezing. To date complete success has been achieved with the lower forms of life only. Sea urchin eggs have been frozen to 14°F, a temperature at which their jelly-like coatings became icy. After being rewarmed, they produced normal tadpoles. Encouraged by this, biologists moved on to fertilized rabbit eggs. Just one out of hundreds survived, and it did not develop beyond the six-cell stage. Rat ova have done slightly better. A group of rat eggs were frozen to −110°F and stored for 6 weeks before defrosting. Nearly all died, but the survivors—about 1 per cent of the total—did mature to the point where they could be implanted into the bodies of female rats. These in time became mothers of normal young.

When freezing of human ova is perfected, it will be possible for a couple to decide whether to have a child with a known set of genes. Tests could identify the most healthy, intelligent, and talented men and women, and their reproductive cells would be saved. As the frozen ova and sperm could last indefinitely, the superior genes would be passed on from one generation to the next.

REPRODUCTION BY WAY OF THE FREEZER

Improperly used, frozen-reproductive-cell banks could present a threat to personal freedom. A powerful group might gain control and determine who may give and who receive sperm or ovum. An international commission, therefore, should be formed to guarantee voluntary use.

A man and woman might then bequeath their reproductive cells to posterity. Information about mental capacity, talents, size, appearance, and health could be fed into a computer and kept in a data bank. The cells would be frozen and stored in liquid nitrogen until there was a call for the traits of their possessors. Then they would be defrosted, and in a laboratory container the sperm would fertilize the ovum, and an embryo would be formed. This embryo could then be implanted in a foster mother's womb. She would, after a normal pregnancy, give birth to a healthy child.

One might ask why anyone would ever agree to have a child in a manner so far removed from love. This method of reproduction could help the woman who, because of some physiological defect, is unable to conceive a child of her own. A husband and wife who carry in their genes an incurable hereditary disease might in this way become the parents of normal children.

In that era, a baby could be born to a woman who is not his mother and fathered by a man unknown to either the person who gives birth or to the true mother.

3. BLOOD, SKIN, AND BONES

Three people in the whole world possess the rare Bombay blood. One of them was discovered when, as a soldier, he contributed to a Red Cross blood drive. The men had been offered a weekend pass in return for a pint of blood. Upon being informed of the unusual typing of this soldier's blood, his superior officers hurriedly had him removed from a combat zone and reassigned as a clerk. They were afraid that he might otherwise be wounded in battle and need transfusions of a kind of blood that could not possibly be provided.

The largest number of people has the blood type O Positive, with A next, followed by B and AB. With the exception of O, which can be

accepted by individuals with some of the other blood types, a person can take a transfusion of his own kind of blood only. Otherwise a severe reaction sets in. This presents an obvious problem to those with rare blood types.

In 1966 a 59-year-old man needed surgery for a stomach ulcer. The operation is not considered a dangerous one, but the patient usually needs two or three blood transfusions. This man's blood type, though, was so unusual that practically any blood but his own would be rejected. The problem seemed impossible to solve, and then his doctors came up with a startling idea: The man would donate his own blood to himself. This had never been done before. The operation was post-poned for several months. The patient came to a doctor's office at regular intervals, and during each visit some of his blood was taken. It was then frozen in order to preserve it for the moment of need. Just before the operation the whole supply of blood was thawed. The patient received all the transfusions he needed—from himself.

Several years later a 4-day-old baby boy lay dangerously ill in Bronx Lebanon Hospital, in New York City. Unless his entire blood supply could be changed, he would suffer severe brain damage or die. The type needed was a U Negative, so rare that it is found in only one of a thousand people. A call went out to the New York Blood Center, which quickly located the right type. Within two hours the rare blood was being transfused into the infant. When he went home a few days later, the doctor reported him as being "in tip-top shape."

Before the spacecraft, Apollo 11, set off on its journey to the moon in the summer of 1969, blood samples were taken from the 250 men and women who worked in the Lunar Receiving Laboratory at Hous-ton. The blood was then frozen and stored to be used later as a basis for comparison with blood taken from the same workers after they had handled material returned from the moon to earth. Could unearthly substances affect humans in such a way as to change the composition of the blood either immediately after exposure or in time to come?

The benefits of freezing naturally affect far more people than those exposed to lunar matter. Until blood was frozen, blood banks operated under the "21-day tyranny." This is how long fresh blood can be kept.

Even with refrigeration, the red cells begin to rupture by then. Vast amounts of blood are wasted. One year 6.4 million pints were donated. Although all of it was needed, 1.7 million pints had to be thrown away. The summer has been the worst time, because so many of the people who donate blood to banks at other seasons of the year go away on vacations. But illness does not take a holiday. Operations go on being performed; women give birth, rivers flood, hurricanes rage, earthquakes break houses apart, wars are fought.

The 21-day tyranny is being overcome by the same liquid nitrogen that saves the sperm for insemination into animals and humans. After 3 minutes in a liquid nitrogen bath, the blood is stored at the cryogenic temperature of $-320°F$. At the time it is thawed for transfusing, the glycerol that has been used to protect it from the cold is removed.

Frozen blood is not intended to replace the fresh altogether. After all, the fresh blood is cheaper. Regular daily requests from hospitals are filled with fresh blood so long as it is available. Thousands upon thousands of pints of frozen blood are being stored for emergency use, and a good part of that supply—about a third—is of rare types. When a person with an uncommon type becomes ill, a blood center can be called. The information about the needed blood is then fed into a computer which quickly locates the right type in any of the banks programmed into it.

Can one pint of blood equal three pints, or four, or more? Anyone knowing arithmetic would say that it could not. But anyone knowing the secrets of freezing would say that it can. In order to do this, the blood is separated into its parts. Each is frozen by itself and a patient needing a transfusion gets only the one he needs, whether it be red cells, white cells, or something else.

Hemophilia, for example, is a peculiar name for a most peculiar blood disease. A minor cut, a tooth extraction, a splinter, a stubbed toe, a severe bruise are extremely dangerous to the hemophiliac; his blood does not clot, but just keeps on flowing. The reason for this is that he lacks the substance in the blood, Factor VIII, which makes the blood of normal people clot. When the method of separating parts of blood for freezing was first worked out, no one could be sure that the process had not damaged the delicate clotting factor. It appeared that a young man on the staff of a blood center was a hemophiliac and he offered himself for experiment. The doctors waited for him to start bleeding; before long he banged his head on a car door and the flow began. The Factor VIII was thawed and injected into him. The factor had survived, and so did the young man.

Victims of leukemia lack another blood segment, the platelets. And these, too, are separated out and given alone.

"Platelets are very fragile and it is extremely difficult to keep them from breaking during freezing," says Dr. Arthur W. Rowe of the New York Blood Center, who has worked out a way of freezing blood. "The priority is being given to children."

Some doctors suggest that anyone with a rare blood type should follow the example of the ulcer patient who froze his own blood while he was still well. Who can say when illness will strike or if surgery will be necessary? A supply of the right type of blood would then always be waiting in the bank.

Everyone has gotten used to the idea of a blood bank, but what of a skin, nerve, muscle, bone marrow, and liver cell bank?

"Virtually every tissue of the body, including nerve and ganglia, has been successfully frozen and revived when protected with 5 to 15% glycerol," reports cryobiologist Dr. Meryman.

But it has not been equally easy to put all of these body tissues to good use. Ideally, it should be possible to use tissues and cells, as blood is used, for transfusions or grafts. But while a person can take someone else's blood, provided that the type is right, he does not accept another's skin or muscle tissue so easily.

The problem lies in the body's ability to recognize which cells belong to it and which do not. This is a very valuable trait, and is under most circumstances essential to health. The system identifies bacteria and viruses as invaders and fights them off vigorously; in this way one recovers from a disease. The body is just as able to determine that a bit of skin, bone marrow, or for that matter, a heart or kidney is foreign and does its best to dispose of them. Certain drugs or x-rays can lessen the violence of the reaction, but even the most drastic medical treatment cannot change the body enough to keep it from rejecting the foreign cells at some time.

But what if each person contributed some of his own cells to the bank when he was healthy? These could be kept in a refrigerated warehouse at an easily reached location. When the need arose, a contributor

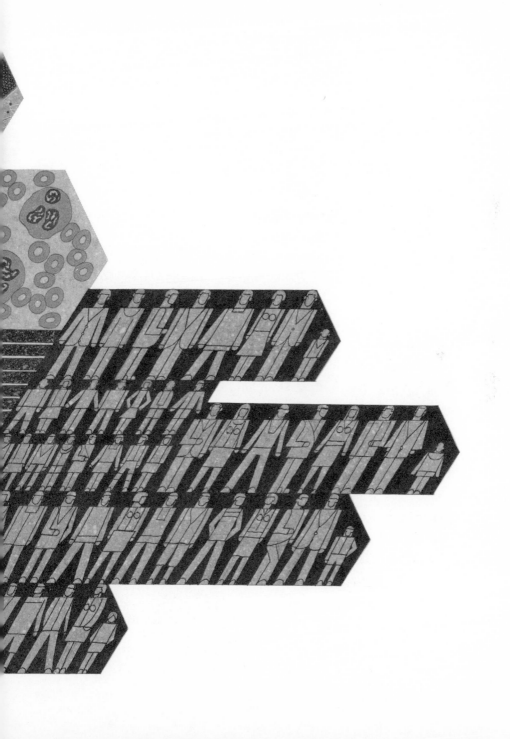

could draw out some of the skin, marrow, or nerve cells he had deposited years earlier. He would never be faced with the difficulty of adjusting to another man's tissues.

Some cells and tissues are frozen in liquid nitrogen, and others are preserved by freeze-drying. Many people are surprised to learn that human and animals cells are freeze-dried, because they connect the process with coffee or meals for campers. It works every bit as well for living tissues. The basic principle for freeze-drying skin, for example, is the same as that used for coffee. The water content of the cell is transformed first into ice and then into vapor without passing through the liquid stage in the middle. This sounds impossible, but it can happen without special equipment under the conditions of everyday life. A housewife hangs her laundry out of doors on a day when the temperature is below 32°F. Shirts and towels are soon stiff with ice. Then the wind blows through and the ice disappears. Yet the cloth does not drip with water. The liquid has turned into gas and disappeared. In the laboratory, cells are first frozen and then placed in a vacuum chamber where drying occurs.

Skin freeze-dried in this way has been used for burn victims. Not long ago a man was trapped in a factory fire and by the time he was rescued, burns covered three-quarters of his body. It was necessary to find some way of covering the burn surfaces so as to guard against infection and further loss of body fluids. Skin is the very best such cover; so water was added to a supply of freeze-dried cells and they were spread, like butter, over the damaged area. After serving as an almost perfect dressing for 21 days, the skin was rejected and peeled off. But by then it had done all that was needed.

Parts of the body that are bloodless can be transferred from one person to another. The cornea of the eye is bathed in a watery fluid instead of blood and so it can be passed from one person to another— or, to be exact, from one dead person to another living, but blind. The cornea can be kept for a week in a refrigerator at 39.2°F. So far, however, efforts to freeze the cornea to temperatures much lower than that have failed.

Freeze-dried heart valves are often used as replacements for those that are damaged. Heart specialist Dr. Brian Barrett-Boyes of Auckland, New Zealand, has gained a world-wide reputation for this kind of transplant. In the late 1960s the wife of an American broadcasting executive travelled all the way to New Zealand to have this operation performed on her.

Another surgeon in Auckland has found an even more unusual use for the freeze-dried heart valves of steers, not humans. These are formed into new eardrums for the deaf. When questioned 6 months after such a transfer operation, one man reported that he could hear well enough to get along with others at work or at a party. Before he had kept to himself, knowing that he could not hear what people were saying.

There are many additional medical applications of freeze-drying. The bite of a cobra, rattlesnake, or mamba brings a fast death unless antivenin serum is given to the victim. Antivenin is now being freeze-dried and sent to desert and jungle places where poisonous reptiles slither along the ground or hang from trees and bushes.

The virus infection of cattle, rinderpest, for centuries was feared, because it would travel from one farm to another until it had destroyed herds throughout a huge continent. The relentless spread could be stopped only by a mass immunization program. Since the virus needed to make the vaccine spoils rapidly at normal temperatures, this was an impossible dream until the coming of cryobiology. Freeze-dried rinderpest virus can now be used to limit the disease.

Polio, once a common cause of death or crippling, is seldom seen in much of the world because of vaccine use. Yet when a physician visited a remote area of South America, he was shocked to see how many people had paralyzed limbs. A local doctor explained to him that there was no refrigeration and stocks of vaccine could not be preserved. Since then thousands of doses have been freeze-dried and distributed for inoculation.

A number of other diseases are also better controlled today because of cold. Influenza is caused by not one, but by many different viruses. As a result the composition of the vaccine that is given to prevent the infection must be changed every so often in order to include the particular viruses present during a given flu season. The illness moves from one country to another, sweeping over oceans and crossing continents. Whenever an outbreak of influenza occurs anywhere, the World Health Organization of the United Nations and its two laboratories—one in Atlanta, Georgia and the other in London, England—must study the virus involved. Then it makes recommendations and sends samples of the germ to health officials all over the world.

"If viruses will be en route longer than 24 hours, they are frozen and shipped on dry ice, or they may be dried," states Dr. Marion T. Coleman who is in charge of the Atlanta laboratory.

Freezing has made the work of medical researchers much easier than it used to be. In the late years of the nineteenth century an American doctor wanted to compare the virus causing the brain inflammation, encephalitis, with another that was being studied in Russia. He wrote to the Russian scientist doing the research and asked for a sample. The Russian responded to the request generously and gave the virus in the only form that was then possible: He infected a tick with the virus and sent the insect along.

Today the researcher could receive a frozen sample of that or any other virus he needed. Practically every microorganism that has yet been identified is stored in a frozen microbe bank, the American Type Culture Collection, in Rockville, Maryland. The bank holds not only those microbes that make humans, animals, and plants sick, but also those that are harmless or beneficial to mankind. In addition, it contains animal cells of a type useful in cancer research, and human cells displaying the abnormalities of mongolism and other birth defects.

In a typical year, scientists withdraw more than 21,500 samples from the Collection. At last count they could choose from among 8000 strains of bacteria, 557 animal viruses and rickettsiae (another type of tiny microbe), 72 plant viruses, about 5300 fungi, 46 algae, and 48 protozoa.

No matter what happens in the future—whether earthquake, hurricane, or man-made disaster—the cells, viruses, bacteria, fungi, algae, and protozoa will be safe in the bank. Most can endure the long periods of cold. Among the fungi, 104 strains have been selected for study. They have survived 5 years of frozen storage. Nor are sexual characteristics of microbes altered. Ten algae strains were carefully tested before and after being frozen and held in liquid nitrogen. Their mating habits were just the same at the end.

Even in the world of nature outside the laboratory where liquid nitrogen temperatures do not occur, there are places cold enough for microbes to be preserved indefinitely. The great British explorer Robert Falcon Scott made his first journey to the Antarctic in 1902. Fifty years later a modern American expedition came upon the remains of one of his old campsites. Scientists pounced upon a glass container with a label—"rising up yeast"—that could barely be made out. The yeast, which is used in baking, belongs to the fungus classification. The bottle was sent to the University of Texas, Austin, where the yeast was removed and studied. After half a century in the Antarctic, it was as capable of growing and making bread rise as it had been on the day Scott left it behind to set off across the polar ice.

The permanence of frozen things is leading sober scientists to suggest a most startling proposal: When a child is born, a tiny bit of his skin, no more than an eighth of an inch, should be taken and frozen and stored. Small amounts of other tissues that can be taken without harm to the baby should be saved. Some cells could be buried in the Antarctic. Fifty, 100, or 500 years from now, the cells can be thawed.

BLOOD, SKIN, AND BONES

Scientists of the future will study them and learn how mankind has changed over the years. What has he done to himself? Have air pollution, water pollution, pesticides, noise, crowding, and radioactive fallout changed the very make-up of the human cell?

4. FREEZING THE DEAD

Who would not wish to live forever? Or if not forever, at least for centuries? This is a dream common to all men. And in the vision of prolonged life, one does not become old, ill, weary, or ugly. The decades go by and do not steal away the handsome face and strong body of youth. The brain does not lose its powers; charm and personality remain.

There are people today who believe that this is not just a dream, but that it lies almost within our grasp.

"Most of us now living have a chance for personal, physical im-

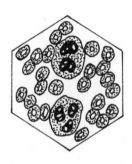

mortality," declares Robert C. W. Ettinger, a former college physics professor, who has founded the movement for freezing the dead.

The first glimmerings of his startling idea came to Ettinger in 1947 when he was lying in a hospital bed recovering from wounds received as a soldier in World War II. He spent his day reading current scientific reports. And among these reports he found a description of experiments being done by Jean Rostand, a French biologist. Rostand had been able to protect frog sperm from freezing injury by adding glycerol. Aside from young Ettinger, bored in his hospital room, no one saw anything of interest in Rostand's discovery. Glycerol did not come into general laboratory use until it was rediscovered by Dr. Audrey Smith. Ettinger, however, grasped the significance at once. In the dry words of the Rostand report, he saw possibilities of the most incredible wonder. He rapidly made the mental jump from frog sperm cells to human beings.

It suddenly struck him that if people were frozen immediately after death, they could be thawed at some time in the future when the disease that had killed them would have been conquered. The cancer victim would awaken only after his disease had been made no more dangerous than inflamed tonsils. The person crippled in an accident would be thawed when his twisted or shrunken limb could be replaced with a perfect one. Or perhaps he would wait out another few centuries until the body could be taught to grow its own replacement parts. The fat and clumsy individual with ugly face and stunted or abnormally large body might return in an era when plastic surgery and hormone treatments had been perfected to the point where they could bring him to his ideal. The retarded and mentally ill would revive when the causes of their conditions were fully understood and easily cured.

The basic plan, as Ettinger saw it, was to keep the dead on ice—or on liquid nitrogen or liquid helium, which are even colder. The frozen corpse would be stored in a freezer at the temperature of these cryogenic gases. He would rest in his icy bed in a state of suspended death as the years and centuries went by. When at last the moment for his revival arrived, his body would be taken from the freezer, thawed, and repaired, and he would live again.

The idea seemed so obvious to Ettinger that he was sure other people would see it, too. But no one did, even after Dr. Smith's work with glycerol in the freezing of sperm was acclaimed. While teaching at Michigan's Highland Park College, Ettinger watched the news and scanned scientific reports. And at last in 1960, he decided that if no one else was going to alert the public to the idea of freezing the dead, he would do so.

He set his theory down in book form and Rostand, his original source of inspiration, wrote the introduction. The book, entitled romantically, *The Prospect of Immortality*, was published in 1962.

That same year, as coincidence would have it, another book on the same subject appeared: *Immortality, Physically, Scientifically Now*, by Ev Cooper.

Although Ettinger and Cooper use the word "immortality" frequently, they do not mean it in the religious sense of an eternal afterlife. They are referring merely to a second period of life on earth. To this end, Cooper had formed an organization, The Life Extension Society, or LES.

The movement, however, needed Ettinger and his more popular book to get it going. More than 400 people joined the LES and offered themselves as advisers to the dying. Followers were found all over the world in countries as widely separated as Venezuela and India. Soon other organizations dedicated to the same aims were formed. Most adopted the name, Cryonics Society, based on the Greek word "kryos" that has entered the English language to stand for extreme cold. Membership in the cryonics societies quickly grew to more than a thousand.

FREEZING THE DEAD

The hope for longer life is as old as thinking man himself, and those who joined the groups were inspired by it. Why should man's time on earth be so short and pass so rapidly? Surely, they reasoned, he should use the intelligence he was given to increase the number of

his days. And at last they saw in cold a scientific way to make this dream a reality.

If we can place the sperm cells into suspended animation and yet bring them back to beget children, if we can freeze the blood and then send it coursing through the veins of living men, if we can chill the yeast cell for half a century or more and still have it make bread rise, if we can cool the encephalitis virus and ship it from continent to continent with all its original powers intact—why not man?

"I have no particular quarrel with your ambition," a leading biologist wrote to the Cryonics Society of New York, "other than that you are more optimistic than the facts warrant."

Man is too complex an organism to respond as sperm and virus do. Not a single higher animal has ever survived freezing to sub-zero temperatures. Although the discovery of glycerol set Ettinger's imagination aflame, cryobiologists believe that it is not really suitable for people. Human beings could not endure the quantities of either glycerol or DMSO that would be needed to guard against freezing damage. The chemicals themselves would be as harmful as the cold.

"Every scientist I've spoken to agrees that freezing a human being successfully is possible," insists Ettinger, but then he adds honestly and regretfully, "Most will say it's possible, but not probable." His own view is that "it is not only possible, but almost certain. The only question is when."

Members of the cryonics societies are not discouraged by the lack of enthusiasm of scientists and by the weight of evidence against freezing and later reviving the dead. Like members of a mystic sect, they have faith. "The only other choice," declares one, "is to let the body decay." And they are only irritated when scientists respond that freezing today is not truly another choice. They agree with Ettinger that even though the freezing techniques are not perfected, "one could freeze the newly dead, accepting whatever degree of freezing damage was unavoidable and still have a non-zero chance of eventual revival."

All damage resulting from the freezing, Ettinger adds, will be taken care of by "our friends of the future." He suggests that the key elements of memory and personality be fed into a computer. With this as a guide, surgeons in the centuries ahead might rebuild parts of the brain "cell by cell, or even molecule by molecule in critical areas." It might take years or even centuries to complete the task, but that would not matter in this golden future.

But would the future really be so golden to those coming from a distant past? They would awaken alone and frightened in a world they could not understand. A man may have been learned and brilliant when last he lived, but compared to the beings in the new era, he might be as one retarded. He would be like a Stone Age savage trying to live in a large American city today.

Ettinger accepts this as a possibility, and says that the reawakened dead might have to live for years in special reservations and take a low place in society while trying to catch up with their new contemporaries. "We could bear this, as we would know that it is only temporary," says Ettinger. "We have the chance of being in time brought up to the level of those around us.

"What is offered is time which gives hope in any situation."

And what of love and family bonds? Will scientists of the future allow a mother, who died of a disease conquered in the next 50 years, to wait for her child dead of a condition it takes 500 years to cure? Can marriage vows survive the freezer? What if a widow remarries? With which husband will she be reunited in the hour of thawing?

The reappearance of past generations would bring about population problems on a scale undreamed of at present. Add the people of today to those of tomorrow and the world would sink beneath the load. Obvious though this appears, the objection does not trouble those dedicated to the idea of freezing. The earth in Ettinger's opinion could hold additional billions of people, and if it became overcrowded, thousands of new planets could be created and some of the overflow be settled in space.

Ettinger does not think that any of these problems need worry people today. He views freezing as a part of medical care, not very different from taking an injection of penicillin or having an operation.

The chief concern of members of the cryonics societies today then is to make sure that they will be frozen. And this is exceedingly difficult to guarantee. Once dead, they are in the hands of others—most of whom are hostile to the idea of freezing.

In 1965 a woman in Springfield, Ohio, lay dying. Her husband had heard about the freezing procedure and decided to arrange for it. Word of the plan leaked out and newspaper reporters rushed to the hospital. While they were waiting, the decision on freezing hung in the balance. The unconscious wife's relatives opposed the plan vigorously. The hospital board would not grant its approval and her doctor refused to take part. When the woman died she was laid to rest in the usual way beneath the earth.

Faced with opposition from hospitals and doctors, the most determined members of the cryonics societies have been training themselves to do the freezing.

After the body has been treated with glycerol or DMSO, it is frozen in dry ice. The corpse may be left in the dry ice for a day or two, and is then transferred to a box or capsule that contains liquid nitrogen. One model that works on the same principle as a thermos bottle has an inner container chilled by liquid nitrogen, an outer container, and a vacuum between the two.

Once the body is frozen and in the container, the question remains what to do with it. One suggestion is to ship all capsules to the Arctic and put them in pits dug in the permafrost layer of the soil that never melts. Others favor the Antarctic. Some cryonics society members feel that the world is not enough and would have bodies shipped to the moon. Not to be outdone, another faction urges the moons of Jupiter.

A simpler and more practical suggestion is to place the containers in refrigerated warehouses on the grounds of cemeteries.

Freezing a body and keeping it frozen indefinitely is a costly business. The capsule alone was $4500 on a recent date. And the liquid nitrogen within and in the warehouse must be regularly replaced. In an effort to put the procedure within the economic reach of the average person, the cryonics societies are turning to insurance. They urge the person who would be frozen to take out a policy for $10,000 or so. Although he—in his frozen state—would actually be the beneficiary, the name on the policy would have to be that of a trusted friend who could be counted on to use the funds for freezing and storage. If no friend or relative is sympathetic, members of the organized groups have volunteered their services.

Ettinger first had his vision in 1947; it was not given a practical application for 20 years. In January of 1967, Dr. James H. Bedford, a retired psychology professor of Glendale City College, California, was close to death from lung cancer. Wanting to be frozen, he was realistic enough to anticipate opposition from hospital administrators. Thus, he entered a private Los Angeles nursing home where freezing equipment had been prepared, and there he died. His physician had been following the failing heartbeats with a stethoscope and the moment they stopped he began to prepare the body for freezing. Members of the local cryonics society rushed to the nursing home to lend a hand. They worked on Dr. Bedford's corpse for the whole day, sending out periodically for more dry ice. The frozen body was then placed in a liquid-nitrogen-filled cryo-capsule for storage.

The greatest fear of those who wish to be frozen is that of dying unexpectedly and alone. Freezing must be started instantly, they believe, or it is too late. For this reason, some of those who would be frozen are particularly careful of themselves during this "first life." But even the greatest of care is not always enough, and accidents do occur. The suggestion has been made that "emergency freezing cards" be carried in the wallet, or a bracelet or dogtag worn. But any of these could be overlooked. Perhaps, say some, the desire for freezing could be tattooed on the body. The only part of the body that is certain to be noticed, however, is the face, and a tattoo there would be an embarrassment at any time except after death. Another possibility is to wear a unit containing a small radio transmitter and battery-powered alarm activated by breathing. Some members of the nearest cryonics society would always be tuned in to the proper frequency ready to rush to the scene at the signal.

No radio signal called helpers to the hotel room in Santa Monica where Marie Phelps-Sweet died suddenly alone and in her sleep on the night of August 26-27, 1967. One of the first LES members in California, she had fervently wanted to be frozen. But everything happened for the worst. Three days passed before word of her death reached members of the freezing societies. Nonetheless, they rushed to the dead woman and began to freeze her already stiff body. Ettinger stayed by the telephone for hours on end, giving advice. Although no one knew if she had left any money, the members took up a collection among themselves and bought the needed supplies.

COLD AGAINST DISEASE

Among Miss Phelps-Sweet's possessions later was found a series of instructions about her own freezing and eventual rewarming. She had enclosed a photograph of herself taken 27 years earlier when she had been a young and lovely woman. "This Is As I Wish To Be Restored!" she had written.

Since then a few other people have been frozen after death. One young man who died of an intestinal ailment in 1968 had left a fund of $200 a year for his postdeath care. He was the first to be frozen at a regular funeral home and stored at an ordinary cemetery. But the number of frozen remains small.

Ettinger and his supporters are quite unable to understand the general indifference to their optimistic plan. They are not looking for any material gain and take no money for giving help, advice, and even freezing supplies on occasion. What they seek is converts. Ettinger would like to be the prophet of a movement that will improve the lot of mankind.

All had been sure that once the method was described, the rush to the freezer would be on. Instead, what has happened? "In the past year or so, many millions have needlessly been buried," Ettinger wrote wearily in a pamphlet. He receives thousands of letters, but relatively few express eagerness to accept freezing for themselves or their families. There is curiosity, rather than action.

What then has gone wrong with freezing the dead? Why has the movement failed to date? The fact is that no one frozen with the techniques known today will ever rise from his capsule to live once more. The frozen dead person is every bit as dead as he who lies buried in the earth. And no amount of wishing can change that inescapable fact.

5. SURGERY WITHOUT SCALPEL

A patient lies on the operating table, his right hand and arm shaking uncontrollably. The surgeon directs a wand tipped with liquid nitrogen into the brain. And all at once, as the icy probe reaches its goal, the trembling stops and does not start again.

This dramatic result is produced by a new kind of operation known as cryosurgery, which literally means cold surgery.

As early as 1883, scientist S. Openchowski had observed that cold kills the brain cells it touches, and only those cells. There is no bleeding and neighboring tissues are not damaged in any way. This is quite

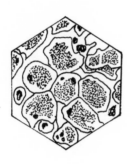

different from the usual kind of surgery with a scalpel cutting through tissues on its way to the target area and causing some bleeding. As happened with Spallanzani, Mantegazza, and many other researchers into cold, Openchowski was ignored. His line of investigation was not picked up again until the late 1940s. Then in the course of the next decade Dr. Irving S. Cooper, a vigorous and attractive young brain surgeon, made the breakthrough that led to cryosurgery.

His intention had been to find a way of relieving the symptoms of Parkinsonism. This disease of the central nervous system afflicts about

1.5 million Americans. It is also called the "shaking palsy," because so many patients have a tremor. Others have a rigid arm or leg that is almost impossible to move or to lift.

"I feel myself to be the victim of a vicious joke," said one victim. "I tremble without cease and without hope of ceasing."

"I am exhausted by the weight of my rigid arm," said another. "Every movement is a herculean task, requiring an enormous effort of will."

For a number of years doctors tried to get at the root of the trouble by operating on the part of the brain which they thought ruled tremors and rigidity. But it proved very difficult to locate that spot exactly enough to stop those nerve impulses and no others. One young musician agreed to the operation, because his arm trembled so that he could not perform. After the surgery his arm could remain still. But he never played again anyway. His personality had undergone a change and he lost all ambition and interest in music. Instead he became a filling-station attendant. Few other cases were quite as dramatic. But many who were operated on complained that even after the tremor or rigidity was relieved, the arm and leg remained weak and partially paralyzed. In the course of the 1940s surgery was performed on 38 Parkinson patients and 25 of them improved.

This relatively mediocre record was clearly related to the fact that surgeons were not reaching the proper location in the brain. If just the right bit of tissue could be destroyed, doctors believed, the unwanted activities would be cut off without causing weakness, paralysis, or changes in personality. Then in 1957 Dr. Cooper became convinced that he had figured out exactly where the area lay that was most responsible for the tremor and rigidity—in the thalamus, a tiny mass of tissue within the brain.

"The word 'talamo' comes from the Greek and its meaning was connubial (marriage) couch," comments Dr. Cooper. "Undoubtedly it was apparent to early investigators that this structure deep within the brain was a hotbed of sensory-motor activity."

Dr. Cooper then designed an instrument, roughly the size of a knitting needle, to carry liquid nitrogen to this site. This narrow wand is insulated throughout its length, so as not to freeze the brain tissue it must pass through on its way to the goal. Only the tip contains the freezing gas. The device came to be known as the "scalpel of ice." He performed his first operations for Parkinsonism with it at St. Barnabas Hospital, New York City, in the early 1960s and the era of cryosurgery was born.

For many, the technique brought new hope. One of the first patients was a lawyer who was frequently embarrassed in court by the tremor in his left arm and leg. During the operation the lawyer, like all undergoing this form of surgery, was fully conscious. He did not suffer, because a local anesthetic was administered for the opening of the skull and the insertion of the wand. From then on the operation was painless, as freezing is of itself anesthetic. The patient remains awake in order to guide the surgeon by his responses to the right spot in his brain. No two people are identical in fingerprints or in thalamus. Any differences in this area are tiny, but they can keep the operation from succeeding.

Cold has added an element of safety to brain surgery that was never there before. Whereas a cut once made cannot be unmade, what is frozen can be thawed. The brain cells are not destroyed immediately; they first go through a stage where they are still living, but inactive. While they are in this state, the surgeon can see what could happen if they were completely frozen. If it does not seem right to him, he can warm the cells and try again.

And so with the tip of the wand resting on his brain tissue, the lawyer was asked to relax his shaking arm. The trembling should have stopped, but it had not. As this was not yet the point of no return, the tip was withdrawn and the chilled part of the brain rewarmed. Then the wand was moved a tiny fraction of an inch. The surgeon watched the arm, and in that instant the shaking stopped.

It is not surprising that cryosurgery came to be called a "miracle cure," although, to be accurate, it is no cure at all. The operation merely removes certain of the effects, such as the tremor; the patient still has the disease.

Two days after the operation the lawyer was out of bed and 5 days later he went home. Shortly thereafter he went back to work. All that was left to show of the surgery was a one-inch scar. "I'll bet I'm the only man you know with a hole in his head," he remarked to one of his clients.

In the next four years Dr. Cooper performed 1800 operations.

Many other surgeons as well began to use the "scalpel of ice." Most, but not all, patients were helped. Comparatively young people and those in whom the disease was progressing slowly showed the greatest improvement.

Several years after the development of cryosurgery, a new drug, Levo-dihydroxyphenylalanine, known popularly as L-dopa, was found to help many patients with Parkinson's disease. Although it often produces severe side reactions, its use has cut down on the practice of cryosurgery as a treatment for Parkinsonism. Dr. Cooper will perform the operation only on those who are not helped by the drug.

Still, far from being abandoned, cryosurgery has gone on to become a recognized and widely used surgical method for a variety of conditions. And its seemingly miraculous "cures" are performed every day. It has proved to be particularly valuable in the relief of diseases that produce uncontrollable muscle movements.

Dystonia and torticollis are singularly unpleasant illnesses that can strike children and young adults. A girl with torticollis sits quietly in a chair and every few minutes her head rolls to her left shoulder. Another looks forever at the ceiling, with head and neck thrown back. A child can be held by dystonia in an awkward position with his back bent strangely. The arms and legs may be shaken by a tremor.

The operation on a 9-year-old boy with this condition was photographed for a national news magazine. The "before" picture showed him with bent back, knotted right leg, and tremors affecting both hands and both feet. The photographer looked on while the wand was inserted in the brain, and suddenly the shaking and spasms on the right side stopped. The boy responded to the surgeon's request that he clench his fist and recite "around the rugged rock the ragged rascal ran" to prove that his speech and mind were not affected. Half an hour later he sat up and hugged his parents. Then he asked for a glass of water and held it without spilling any, which he had been unable to do before.

Different parts of the thalamus may be involved in a variety of disease symptoms, so it is sometimes necessary to operate several times to reach them all. This is the case when both sides of the body are affected, as was true of the 9-year-old boy. Nonetheless, patients, par-

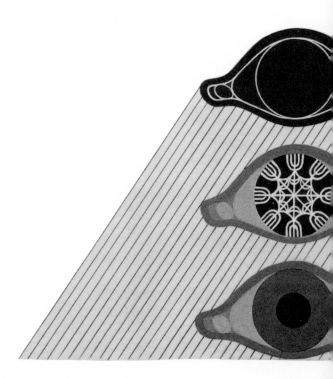

ticularly young ones, are able to endure the surgery very well. One boy who underwent four operations on the thalamus later went to Yale University and was graduated with high honors.

As cryosurgery came into wider use, physicians began to try it as a treatment for cancer. They hoped that cold would destroy cancer cells —just as it does brain cells—without affecting nearby healthy tissues. It turned out to be much more difficult to kill cancers than to destroy tiny bits of the thalamus. Surgeons discovered that it was necessary to freeze the cancer cells, thaw them, freeze them again, and repeat the whole process several times. Thawing does considerable damage to the cancer cells. The ice crystals that form inside the cells during freezing get a little bigger just before they melt. They push against the cell membrane and injure it. When finally frozen, the cancer shrinks into a bloodless, solid mass. It can be taken out, or if it is not pressing painfully against some organ or nerve, can be left where it is.

The cryoprobe, the term doctors use for the "scalpel of ice," can be inserted with only a local anesthetic, which is an advantage for the elderly or those with heart disease. Such people may not be able to endure complete anesthesia. When a heart patient developed a cancer of the lip, the probe was inserted and the cancer frozen in six places to a temperature of $-292°F$. The patient's only complaint was that he had a burning sensation. Within a few days the frozen cells began to peel off. A month later he looked in the mirror and, peer as he would, could see no trace of where the wound had been.

The cryoprobe can reach cancers—and also noncancerous but dangerous tumors—that are hard or even impossible to approach with the standard scalpel.

A tumor can be lodged so deep within the brain that cold becomes a last hope. A few years ago a middle-aged man entered St. Barnabas Hospital suffering from terrible headaches and convulsions. The tumor within his brain had a jelly-like consistency that would formerly have made it quite impossible to handle. At the touch of the cryoprobe, however, it froze into a solid mass that stuck to the tip and was pulled out. Two weeks later the patient left the hospital. Soon thereafter an operation was performed on a 16-year-old girl whose sight was threatened by a tumor pressing on the optic nerve. The growth was so large that the probe had to be moved five times. The girl recovered rapidly and did not lose her sight.

Diseases of the prostate gland, located at the base of the bladder in men, are common among the elderly, and surgery is often needed both for cancerous and noncancerous conditions. Liquid nitrogen can freeze the entire prostate in about 2 minutes. If there are no complications, a skillful surgeon can insert the wand, freeze the tissues, and withdraw the instrument in a mere 10 minutes.

After a rather large number of prostate operations had been performed, something happened that may prove to have great significance for the future of cryosurgery and of cancer. In 1965, a 65-year-old man was treated cryosurgically for prostate cancer at Millard Fillmore

Hospital in Buffalo, New York. By the time of the operation the cancer had spread to his lungs. This is not an uncommon side effect of this disease; cancer cells from the prostate can spill out and travel through the system. When this man came back for a checkup several months later, it was discovered that not only the prostate cancer, but also the cancer in the lungs was gone. At that time it was assumed to be a coincidence.

Then 3 years later the same thing happened again with two more patients whose cancers had spread from the prostate to their lungs or vertebrae. The first man was also still alive.

Why did it happen? The answer may lie in changes in the body's ability to throw off cancerous tissues. Certain substances, the cancer antigens, are present in normal people and help them to fight off cancer. These antigens are lacking in the cancer patient. Perhaps, suggests Dr. Richard J. Ablin, Director of Immunology at Fillmore, the cryosurgery affects the prostate in such a way as to cause it to release the needed antigens into the bloodstream.

Despite its apparent victories, doctors warn that cryosurgery should not be considered a cure for cancer. One must not overlook the fact that many cancers fail to be destroyed by cold, no matter how it is applied. And even when the patient appears to have recovered, it is much too early to say for sure that he will not relapse some time in the future. Liquid nitrogen can be considered as one more weapon in the battle against cancer, a battle that has not yet been won.

SURGERY WITHOUT SCALPEL

The ability of the wand to reach otherwise unreachable sites within the body is of value in treating a number of all but incurable conditions, aside from cancer. The pituitary gland is no bigger than a pea, yet it plays a tremendous part in the development of sexual characteristics and body size. If it functions improperly a dainty girl may be transformed into an almost manly one. In other persons, the hands, feet, and face can become huge or the entire body can grow to gigantic proportions. The pituitary is enclosed in bone and attached to the base of the brain, so it is extremely difficult for a surgeon to get in there with a scalpel and correct the condition. Only a tiny opening in the bone is necessary, however, for the tip of the cryoprobe to pass through and deliver its burden of cold. The pituitary resists cold so vigorously that it takes 15 minutes for the harmful tissues to be destroyed.

The fact that freezing does not cause bleeding makes it a valuable technique whether the condition being treated is an overactive pituitary, cancer, or a less major, but still troublesome condition. A small boy needed to have his tonsils removed a year or two ago. This is, as most children know, a minor operation—uncomfortable, but seldom serious. The problem was that this youngster was suffering from a blood disorder, and could not afford to lose any blood. His tonsils were, therefore, frozen out with liquid nitrogen, and no blood at all flowed. So far tonsil freezing has not yet replaced the standard tonsillectomy, except in such cases, but it in time may become the standard method.

COLD AGAINST DISEASE

Liquid nitrogen was used for the first time to kill tiny tumors on the larynxes, or voice boxes, of several infants in 1960. This success brought an unexpected bonus: The report was read by Dr. Cooper who was then looking for a suitable refrigerant for his probe.

A stage actor had been unable to get movie or television work because the merciless eye of the camera revealed warts on his face. Nine of them were frozen off at one time, leaving no scar for eye or camera to see.

Acne, which is sometimes known as the "curse of adolescence," can leave marks on the face. The scars can be partially wiped out by freezing the skin and then removing the top layer with a rotating brush.

A young man woke up one morning to find that he had allowed a hideous picture to be tattooed on his arm after a party the night before. He was much relieved to learn that freezing would get it off.

If cold can remove a tattoo or wart from the skin, might it not take a cataract from the eye? The cataract, an opaque film over the lens of the eye, is the leading cause of blindness in the old. The question whether cold could help was asked in the early 1960s by young Dr. Charles Kelman. Just as Dr. Cooper's name is linked with freezing of the thalamus, Dr. Kelman's is linked to that of the eye.

Dr. Kelman likes to remark that he might never have made his discovery at all. After he worked his way through medical school as a writer of popular songs, he toyed with the idea of giving up medicine and becoming a composer instead. But the attraction of the medical profession proved too strong to resist and he became an ophthalmologist, a doctor specializing in the eye. One day while waiting for his wife to finish dressing so that they could go out to the movies together, he started to thumb through a magazine. It contained an article about Dr. Cooper and his scalpel of ice. Dr. Kelman began to wonder whether he might find in cold a way of removing cataracts. He joined Dr. Cooper at St. Barnabas and began to work out this problem.

The principle that Dr. Kelman applied was an extremely simple one that can be observed in everyday life: A cold metal sticks to a moist object. And so the cataract sticks to the cryoprobe and comes away from the eye.

After doing experiments on rabbits and cats, Dr. Kelman performed his earliest cataract operations on humans in late 1962 and his paper on this accomplishment appeared in January of 1963. Dr. Kelman had believed that he was the first person in the world to have found this use of cold, and was disappointed to learn that Dr. Tadeusz Krwawicz in Lublin, Poland, had been freezing cataracts since 1961. He took comfort from the fact that Dr. Krwawicz had used a metal probe dipped into a mixture of dry ice and alcohol, which was less efficient and effective than Dr. Kelman's device.

Dr. Kelman had started with Dr. Cooper's liquid nitrogen cryoprobe, but as cataracts need to be only partially frozen, the cryogenic gas was not really necessary. He replaced the liquid nitrogen with plain water and designed a device that could be plugged into any wall outlet. Low temperatures are created by means of what scientists call the Peltier effect. "When a direct current is passed through the junction of two dissimilar semiconducting metals," explains Dr. Kelman, "the junction becomes cold and the terminals hot."

The water-cooled cryostylet, as he named the tiny instrument, can achieve the temperature range of 24.8° to −22°F that is needed for cataract removal. After the cataract has been lifted off, the patient needs to spend just one day in bed, a week in the hospital, and 2 weeks in a rest home. Then he is fitted with special glasses or contact lenses and can return to a normal, active life.

Although cataracts occur most often in the old, they are occasionally found in young people, too. Cataract operations on the young are far more difficult, because the spokes holding the lens (and cataract) in the eye are so strong. Dr. Kelman still recalls an operation performed on a 9-year-old girl. It took him 5 minutes to break the spokes and remove the ice ball of cataract and tissue.

The success with cataracts led physicians to look into the possibility of using cold to treat other eye conditions. Sometimes, for reasons that are still unknown, the retina of the eye becomes split off or detached from the neighboring layer. The space between is filled with fluid and vision is damaged. A cure involves stimulating the eye to produce a physiological "glue" strong enough to fasten the retina back in place. Cold is one of the best and fastest ways of encouraging this glue production. An ophthalmologist in Houston, Texas, recently reported that he had used cold to "spot weld" 520 detached retinas back into place.

Medicine has come a long way since the sixteenth and seventeenth centuries in terms of putting parts of the body back together again. In those days the noble art of dueling over a fair lady often resulted in the detachment of the tip from the nose or the curve from the cheek. The injured swordsman would take the severed bit in his hand and run as fast as he could to the nearest apothecary to have it stitched back on.

6. AN END TO PAIN

A high school baseball player runs for a ball in the outfield. He misjudges the distance, and is hit by the ball. What will relieve the pain of the bruise and put him back on the team rapidly? The American Medical Association Committee on the Medical Aspects of Sports suggests that an ice pack be applied to the injured area immediately after the accident. This treatment should be repeated as many times as possible over the next 24 to 48 hours. Once the bruise has begun to swell and discolor, the advice is to try heat and put on warm compresses. Some doctors go farther than that in championing cold. They

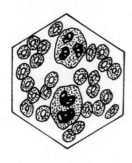

recommend that cold and only cold be applied until pain and swelling are reduced, no matter how long that takes.

Who does not know the relief from pain that cold can bring? Press ice cubes against a cut or mosquito bite and it does not hurt so much. A cold compress relieves a sprained ankle. An ice bag is held to the aching head.

The discovery that cold could relieve suffering was made long before the era of modern medicine. Two-and-a-half thousand years ago Greek physicians chilled the bodies of people afflicted with tetanus. In the days before the tetanus vaccine this terrible infection could follow a cut with a rusty nail or weapon. As its common name, "lockjaw," reveals, the victim's mouth was sometimes locked shut by the muscular contraction produced by the disease. The chilling did not bring a cure, but it eased the misery.

Rabies or hydrophobia, which can enter the system in a bite from a rabid dog, was one of the most terrifying of all diseases before a vaccine was discovered. The famed Roman doctor, Aulus Cornelius Celsus, author of a nine-volume encyclopedia on medicine, recommended that those stricken with hydrophobia be dunked in icy cold water. The reasoning of the Romans of the first century A.D. was based on superstition rather than science. They believed that the patient had been possessed not by a germ, but by a demon. The freezing water would scare out the demon and he would flee. The chilling could not hold off the madness and death that are the end-results of hydrophobia, but again, must have relieved the agony a bit.

To seek the origin of cold's use as a pain-killer one must go farther back in history than the ancient Romans and Greeks. The faded hieroglyphics of an Egyptian papyrus drawn in 2500 B.C. or earlier shows cold being applied to wounds and infections. This practice was passed on from one generation to the next and then forgotten for a time.

The casualties among the men in the French Grand Army were high during Napoleon's ill-fated campaign to Russia early in the last century. Many were wounded so badly that arms and legs had to be amputated on the spot. Seeking a way to make the pain endurable

82

without anesthesia, Baron Dominique Jean Larrey, the surgeon accompanying the army, looked helplessly over the snow-covered field. All at once he realized that there lay his anesthetic. He ordered wounded arms or legs to be packed in snow before amputation.

The first truly scientific observations on cold anesthesia were made by a Britisher, Dr. James Arnott, who started his career as physician on the *Lady Campbell* voyaging between Britain and the Bengal in India. Bored with life at sea, Dr. Arnott became superintendent of the East India Company's Medical Estate of St. Helena. This, too, failed to excite him for long, and in 1835 he returned to England on a furlough and went into practice in the seaside resort of Brighton. Soon he began to experiment with the pain-killing uses of cold. When about to start an operation, he would take a pig's bladder, fill it with lukewarm water, place it against the area to be operated on, and then drop in ice. After 15 or 20 minutes the patient had no feeling at all in that part of his body and Dr. Arnott would make the first cut.

Although one might expect a man so interested in anesthesia to be a warm and kindly person, Dr. Arnott was anything but that. He thought of his patients as if they were guinea pigs on which he could practice his theories. One day he set out to convince his fellow doctors that cold really did reduce pain. He invited a number of doctors to be present while he operated on a young woman who had several small tumors. First he applied the freezing bladder and then removed one of the growths. All present could see that the operation had been painless. Then Dr. Arnott waited for the tissues to warm up and removed another tumor. As the woman screamed in agony, Dr. Arnott had the satisfaction of knowing that he had proved his point. His research, however heartless, did benefit his patients most of the time. He was the first to report on the fact that cold could relieve the pain of cancers located at the neck of the uterus in women. Dr. Arnott was not a charlatan and was careful not to claim a cancer cure.

By the nineteenth century all sorts of devices for employing cold had been made. An Englishman, Thomas Masters, invented an ice machine intended for the making of ice cream, but then he had a bright idea of how to sell even more machines and more ice. He described this glowingly in *The Ice Book,* published in 1844. And although he exaggerated, his basic plan is sound: "In numberless cases where extreme thirst, prostration of strength, restlessness, total want of sleep, and raving delirium prevailed, the application of ice-cooled water to the whole body by a sponge slaked the thirst, roused the strength, calmed the patient, dispelled the delirium, and induced sleep from which the sick arose refreshed and comfortable."

Fourteen years later, Dr. R. E. Harrison presented another invention in a book with a title that gives away its entire contents: *What is Congelation? or the Benumbing Influence of Cold in Producing Insensibility to Pain in Dental Operations Popularly explained with remarks on the introduction of a "Painless System" in Dental Surgery.*

Proud of the era in which he lived, Dr. Harrison believed that no one in the past could possibly have known how to use cold: "The *idea* that cold produced insensibility to pain has been floating about for ages," he wrote. "The principle was known, frozen up in the minds of men, but wanting the vivifying (life-giving) influence of the nineteenth century to thaw it into a practical channel."

One result of the "thaw" was Dr. Harrison's hollow mouthpiece through which a freezing fluid was passed. The frigid mouthpiece was placed on the gum and was large enough to cover the teeth. When the the area was completely numb, Dr. Harrison extracted the tooth. Like other doctors using cold, he observed that bleeding as well as pain was reduced.

The ultramodern device frightened some of his patients. One young girl took a look at the equipment and headed for the door shrieking, "Oh, I won't be *numbed,* I don't want numbing." A more sophisticated young lady, however, wrote him a thank-you note: 'Miss _____ presents her compliments to Mr. Harrison, and begs to assure him that after experiencing the ease and comfort of that method of extracting teeth. . . ."

Harrison and Baron Larrey have their modern counterparts. Some doctors chill limbs of those unable to stand anesthesia in dry ice or ice water, rather than snow gathered from the fields. A large synthetic rubber boot that is cooled by the circulation of a combination of alcohol and water has just been designed in the University of Wisconsin's laboratories in Madison. The patient puts on the boot and keeps it on until the leg is completely without sensation; then the operation can be performed.

Upon learning of the cooling boot, a football coach asked if his players could use it when hurt during a game. As the AMA Committee has found, the cooling reduces the swelling rapidly and efficiently. Six injured football players were soon thereafter treated in this way.

Dr. Arnott had soothed cancer pain by applying cold to the outside of the body. But many cancers are located far below the surface. Today, with sophisticated medical techniques, it has become possible to deliver cold deep within the body. While the question remains whether cryosurgery is a cure for cancer, it does appear to be remarkably effective in relieving pain. The liquid nitrogen destroys the free sensory nerve endings in and around the cancerous growth, so that they cannot transmit the message of pain.

A woman came to the Sloan-Kettering Institute for Cancer Research, New York City, in agony from a cancer on her neck. The liquid nitrogen failed to destroy the growth and the woman died of it soon afterwards. But the freezing did succeed in controlling her suffering, and she spent her last days calmly.

Another patient was in extreme pain, as a cancer of the ear extended inward to the mastoid bone. Surgeons cut away as much of both tumor and bone as they could, and then applied the cryoprobe. So far this man has remained free not only of pain, but of the cancer as well.

As cryosurgery has been effective in removing cataracts and repairing detached retinas, ophthalmologists tried it on another illness of the eye, glaucoma. The disease produces an increase in the amount of aqueous humor, the fluid within the eyeball. This builds up a painful pressure against the retina. Glaucoma can produce a variety of prob-

lems ranging from minor difficulties in seeing properly to total blindness. Some physicians believe that the extreme cold of the probe reduces the flow of liquid and so relieves the pressure. Dr. Kelman, who perfected the technique, disagrees and is quick to point out that the probe will not cure blindness, if the disease has progressed to that point. "Cryosurgery is of help in hopeless cases of glaucoma," he adds, "only because it can make a blind eye less painful." Whatever else it may achieve then, this benefit of cold is certain.

The ultimate use of cold as a pain-killer was worked out in the 1960s by Dr. Melville Roberts and Dr. William M. Chadduck of the University of Virginia School of Medicine, Charlottesville. At that time freezing had become an accepted treatment for Parkinsonism, and they speculated on what would happen if Dr. Cooper's cryoprobe were inserted not into the thalamus, but into the frontal lobe of the brain which affects the body's reaction to pain. Since cryosurgery permits exact tissue destruction, they could kill the specific nerve cells involved in giving pain its emotional impact without damaging other cells.

For their first patients they chose two men and a woman, each with an intensely painful condition. All suffered to such an extent that even huge doses of drugs brought little or no relief.

Although the target area was different, the operation was similar to that for parkinsonism or dystonia. Each patient remained awake throughout, so as to answer questions and respond to instructions. As with the thalamus, there is a margin for error. If the person begins to talk, look, or move strangely, the probe can be withdrawn and the cells warmed up. The wand is then reinserted a little way off.

Each of these first three patients gradually became indifferent to his suffering. "I feel the pain, but it doesn't matter," one of them told the surgeon.

This happy mood lasted long afterwards. None of them was worried or depressed. Although they continued to be aware of the pain, they remained untroubled by it. Drugs were not called for. All three returned home and lived with their families in relative comfort until the end.

7. WHEN CHILLING HEALS

During the twelfth century when Richard the Lion Hearted of England was leading the Third Crusade against the Moslems, he was stricken with a fever. Upon learning of this, his enemy, the Sultan Saladin, known as much for gallantry as courage, ordered his soldiers to travel to the distant mountains with a caravan of camels. The men gathered snow on the mountain tops and packed it in skin gourds, fastened them to the camels' backs, and returned to Saladin. Careless of his safety, Saladin entered Richard's camp carrying the snow-filled gourds. The surprised Crusaders, recognizing the generous nature of the act, stood by while Saladin and his soldiers packed the sick man in the snow.

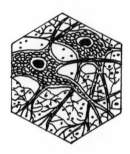

Soon the fever went down and Richard recovered and returned to the battle.

The story, a part of the romance that has been woven about these two great opponents, lived on. But the lesson that might have been drawn from it was not. And so it has been over the years. Legends, epics, yellowed documents, and old medical reports reveal that the value of cold has been discovered quite independently in one country after the other. The role of pain-killer is only one of the many medical parts it can play. While some early physicians used cold for diseases, such as rabies, which it could not possibly cure, others applied it to conditions that do respond to chilling. The knowledge has been lost, only to be found again time after time.

In ancient China the physician Ch-Hua t'o had a great reputation. Whenever a patient with a fever consulted Ch-Hua t'o, he was promptly stripped and carried to a stone trough in the garden where icy water was poured on him. This is known today, because in the third century A.D., Ching Chung-ching, a follower of the great Ch-Hua t'o, described this treatment. His essay, however, had little influence, and was forgotten for hundreds of years.

On a winter's day, Dr. Thomas Sydenham, a prominent British physician of the seventeenth century, entered the room of a desperately sick man, threw open the windows, and dipped the bedsheets in cold water. The patient and his family were stunned; other doctors were shocked. But the man lived and Dr. Sydenham went right on chilling patients. As quite a number of them recovered, several other doctors quietly followed his example. This was, to be sure, an era before antibiotics and other modern drugs, and patients with high fevers often died. Drastic measures, therefore, were justified.

In 1767, Dr. William Wright, a British naval doctor, caught a tropical illness while his ship was cruising near the Bahama Islands southeast of Florida. Feeling as if he were burning up, he staggered onto the deck for a breath of air. While he stood on the deck, a high wave swept over the side of the vessel and drenched his entire body. Dr. Wright had never heard of cold water as a medical treatment, so he had no reason to expect the result: His temperature dropped and he felt considerably better. For the next few days Dr. Wright insisted that the sailors pour sea water over him. They did so, although they clearly thought it an insane idea. In later years Dr. Wright used cold in his medical practice, chiefly as a treatment for malaria. He then published a report on his work.

Several years later a Scottish doctor, James Currie, living in Liverpool, England, happened upon Dr. Wright's report. At that time a typhoid epidemic was raging in Liverpool and Dr. Currie was searching for a new kind of treatment. Dr. Wright's paper gave this to him. He ordered patients to sit in tubs of icy water. Many of them got better.

But Dr. Currie went a step farther than Dr. Wright or than Saladin, for that matter, and performed experiments to discover what chilling really did to the body. He was one of the earliest physicians to make use of the mercury thermometer and it was for years thereafter to be known as "Currie's thermometer." The normal temperature range of healthy people was noted and then used as a basis for comparison with temperatures of the sick. Dr. Currie recorded the effects of cooling not only on body temperature, but also on heartbeat, breathing, and other physiological activities. He was thus the first to observe that hypothermia, the name given to the dropping of body temperature to below 95°F, slows down most body functions. And this is the reason why cooling helped the typhoid victims whom Dr. Currie treated. They did not feel better because the germs in their bodies were killed by the cold. Indeed, bacteria, viruses, and other microbes are far better able

93

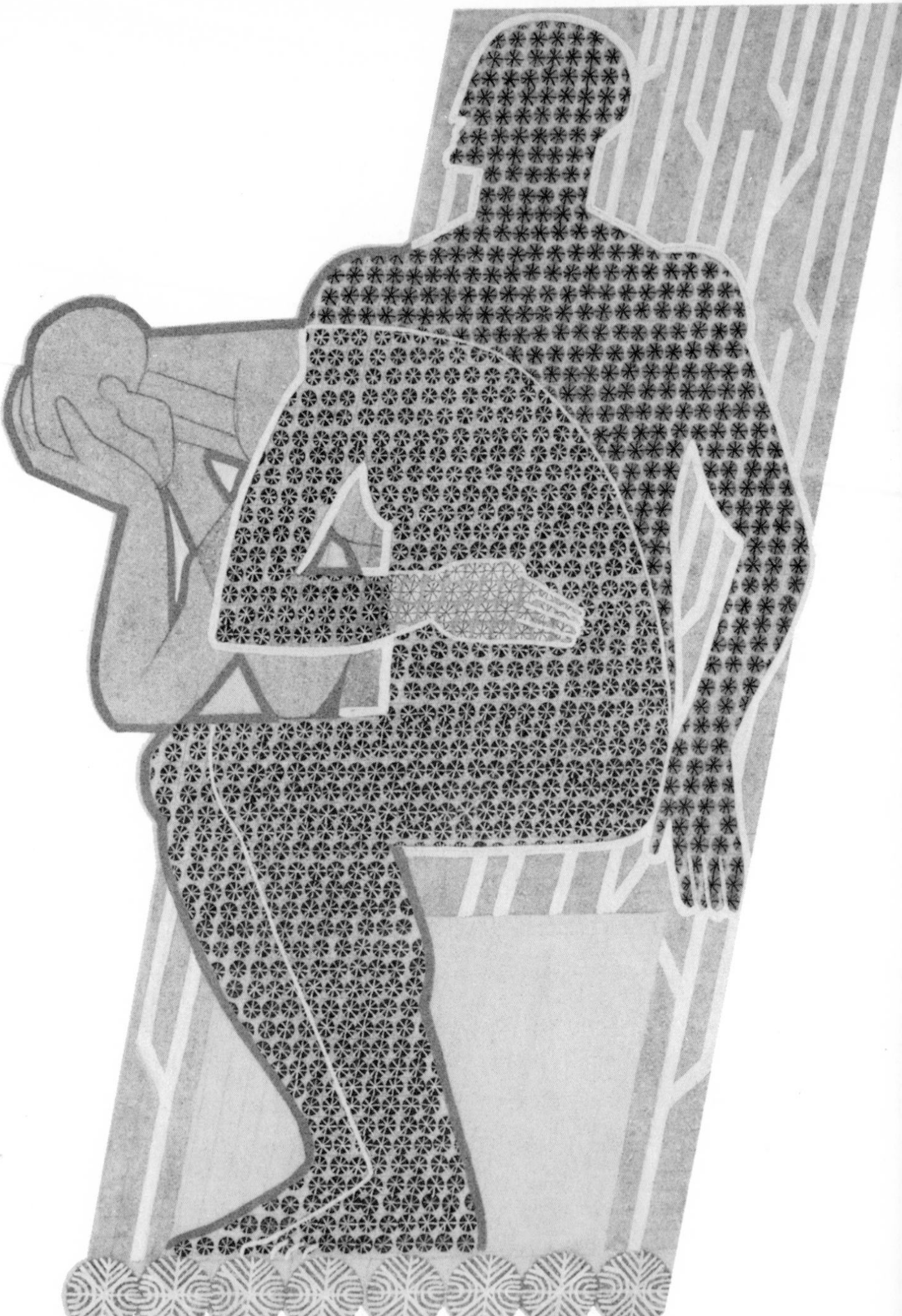

to withstand cold than more highly developed organisms. The patients improved, because their physiological needs were reduced to manageable proportions. Hypothermia does not actually cure any disease. It merely saves the patient's strength and in this manner helps him to fight off illness.

Why is this so? When the body is cooled to about 10 degrees below normal, metabolism slows to roughly half its normal rate. As the system works less vigorously, its need for oxygen is dramatically decreased. By the time the temperature is down to 78°F, the lungs take in between one-fourth and one-fifth of the quantity of air they would use at normal temperature. The heart naturally pumps much more slowly. At 82.4°F the rate is down to 58 per cent of normal. The blood courses sluggishly through the veins, like a river flowing through a mudbank.

What could this mean to a person who is dangerously ill? The strain on his heart and lungs is greatly reduced. When surgery is required, he bleeds less. His brain, kidneys, digestive tract, and other body systems are given what amounts to a vacation and can rest.

The first modern doctor to follow the methods of Dr. Currie and Ch-Hua t'o was Dr. Temple Fay, who in November of 1938 packed crushed ice around the chest, arms, and legs of one of his patients. Then he opened the windows of the room and let in the chilly autumn air. The body temperature soon fell to between 88° and 90°F, and was maintained at this level for 4 days.

In 1939, Dr. Fay's report on this and other cases appeared under the title, "Observations on Prolonged Human Refrigeration." The manuscript unluckily fell into the hands of the Germans, who were then performing medical research using concentration camp prisoners as unwilling guinea pigs. Research was merely an excuse for methodical cruelty. The Nazis planned an experiment based on the Fay report. They set out to discover how low the body temperature had to fall to kill a man. Eight inmates of the infamous Dachau concentration camp were placed in a tank of water that had been chilled to exactly 39.2°F. There they stayed until death came. Their temperatures were taken at regular intervals. Most of the prisoners died after 65 minutes in the water, and their body temperatures just before death varied from 75.6° to 84.2°F. One man, however, managed to last for nearly 3 hours, with a body temperature of 77.4°F. These findings are not very valid, in any event, as the concentration camp prisoners were close to death due to starvation and mistreatment.

Despite this tragic misuse of hypothermia, in the years after the Nazis were defeated, it has made an important place for itself in modern medicine. Ways of lowering body temperature have been refined only recently. The crude system of dunking a man or woman in a tub of ice water, as was done by Ch-Hua t'o and only slightly changed by Dr. Currie, survived into the age of wonder drugs. Today, however, techniques less shocking to the patient are used. He may be cooled with ice packs placed all over the surface of his body, or he may lie in a box through which cold air circulates. In the method used most often today, the person is placed on a specially constructed mattress or is covered with a rubber or plastic blanket. A frigid solution is passed through tubes set within mattress or blanket.

WHEN CHILLING HEALS

Hypothermia is an unnatural state and the body fights to retain its normal temperature. Severe bouts of shivering and sometimes convulsions may occur. These can be controlled and the ordeal of chilling made easier by the use of certain drugs. This was observed in 1961 by a French doctor, H. Laborit, and he is usually considered the originator of this method. A study of history, though, proves this to be incorrect. As early as the second century A.D. the physician Galen, who lived in Rome, wrote that a number of medicines have a "refrigerant effect" and can help to cool the body.

The sedatives given to a mother during childbirth cross the placenta and enter the bloodstream of the infant. Some of the drugs remain in the baby's system and so it is easy to reduce his temperature. Even without medication, infants cannot fight off hypothermia the way adults do. The heat-regulating system of their bodies is too immature to work very well.

Years ago, particularly in rural areas, midwives often delivered babies at home. If an infant had trouble in breathing at birth, the midwife would place him in a basin of cold water. Frequently this brought him around. The method fell into disfavor with the passage of time and the move from home to hospital. Then in the 1960s the Pediatric Society in Finland reported that 100 newborns with breathing problems had been cooled and had improved. A number of these babies were checked repeatedly over the next year or two to see whether they were developing normally. It is known that the brain can be damaged if it does not receive its normal supply of oxygen. On the average, these babies stood up before they were 10 months old, spoke their first words at a year, and began to walk a month later. The cooling had probably protected their brains. Chilling, as has been observed, reduces the need for oxygen to the point where the weak breathing of a sickly, frail newborn could provide enough. The midwives in the old days certainly had not known this when they called for the basin of cold water.

Despite its many successes, cold has not gained general acceptance as a treatment for the premature. Some doctors point out that chilling to a temperature below 89.6°F can of itself injure an infant. Prematures are, therefore, usually placed in heated incubators—and most survive this practice, too.

Taking a lesson from the experiences of Dr. Sydenham and Dr. Currie, some physicians today are cooling the seriously ill. Septic shock is an extremely dangerous condition that sometimes follows a bacterial or viral infection. Body demands for oxygen and nutrients increase to the point where they cannot be satisfied. Even if treated with antibiotics, septic shock frequently leads to death. When the body is cooled and its demands lowered, the patient's chances improve. In one hospital 35 out of 59 people chilled for septic shock recovered. This may not sound good, but it is more than twice the average number of survivors from this condition.

Staphyloccal pneumonia is another disease that carries a high death rate. Patients are usually kept warm. This practice is challenged by research on mice performed by Dr. Ian M. Smith of the University of Iowa College of Medicine, Iowa City. He infected white mice with the germ and then warmed them. A large number died. Then he took other sick mice and placed them in a refrigerator where the temperature was 39.2°F. This group lived about 2 hours longer than a third group of mice which was neither warmed nor cooled. Such treatment is still in the experimental stage and many doctors do not believe that humans will react as the animals did.

The most dramatic modern use of hypothermia occurred in the 1950s when the French were conducting the war in Indo-China. Severely wounded young soldiers frequently went into shock, a condition characterized by a general physiological collapse. Many died of this before they could be taken to a hospital behind the lines for treatment. Army doctor Lieutenant Colonel C. Chippaux then suggested: "Place the men in artificial hibernation."

This picturesque term is the European way of describing hypothermia. In keeping with Lieutenant Colonel Chippaux' instructions, the body temperature of each of a group of injured men was lowered. The "hibernating" French soldiers were taken to hospitals far from the battlefield. During this entire period cold kept them from going into shock. In addition, they lost less blood from their wounds than they otherwise would have done. A cold body does not bleed much, as anyone who has ever applied ice to an open cut has learned. A surprisingly large number of these chilled soldiers survived.

There were a few mistakes, however. Sometimes the doctor who had placed the soldier in "hibernation" would not be able to get in touch with the hospital. Communications breakdowns are, after all, common enough in wartime. The "hibernating" soldier would then arrive unannounced, seeming half dead, with a slow heartbeat and shallow breathing. The doctor who examined him might be overworked and exhausted. And so sometimes a false diagnosis was made and the man received improper treatment.

Still, on the whole the system worked well in the winter. Then came the summer. The thermometer climbed to 104°F and higher. Refrigeration and air conditioning, even ice, were not available near the front. There was no way of keeping the soldiers cold enough to maintain "hibernation" during the long trip behind the lines to the hospital.

Whatever the drawbacks to using hypothermia under battle conditions in Southeast Asia, Lieutenant Colonel Chippaux had made a valuable medical contribution: He had proved that cold could provide protection against shock following injury. Accidents occur in peacetime, too, in temperate climates and countries where victims can be carried in air-conditioned planes, trains, and cars.

8. SAFETY IN COLD

On a winter's day in 1740 a workman fell off a scaffold to his death. His body was taken to a hospital where an autopsy was performed. When the doctor, Jeannes Baptista Morgagni, opened the skull, he noticed that the brain had changed in a number of ways. There was no swelling; the texture was surprisingly firm, and the blood vessels were closed off. After casting about for an explanation, he could think of only one: The room in which he had been working was unheated. The cold air must have produced these effects on the dead brain.

This is precisely what happens to the chilled living brain, too. Inflammation, swelling, and bleeding are reduced. Not long ago a

young man was brought to a hospital after his car had gone out of control and hit a tree. His brain had been damaged. Doctors hastened to lower his temperature to between 92° and 90°F and did not let it rise for some days. Then he was rewarmed, and recovered.

Cooling is equally useful in nonaccidental head injuries, such as brain surgery. Therefore, patients frequently are chilled during and after operations on the brain.

As the chilled brain gets slightly smaller in size, the surgeon is able to deal with abnormalities on the brain surface that cannot be reached when the brain is its normal size. Five patients at Columbia–Presbyterian Medical Center in the City of New York had defects of the large surface blood vessels. They were of a type that doctors usually describe as "unapproachable." Yet when these people were cooled to about 84°F their brains shrank enough to make successful surgery possible.

The benefits of cooling for brain surgery go beyond the reduction in bleeding and swelling. A drop in the metabolic rate may save the patient from life as a human vegetable. It does not take much time at normal temperature to destroy the brain forever. Just 3 to 5 minutes without blood, and intelligence is lost. But when the brain is cooled only a little—to 86°F—the mind is not affected for a safety period lasting from 8 to 10 minutes. And the colder it gets, the longer it can remain without oxygen and blood.

The brain is in danger during operations that would seem to have nothing to do with it. In the course of heart or lung surgery, the flow of blood to the brain may be interrupted. Fortunately, the cooling procedure that protects these organs protects the brain as well.

The open-heart operation was developed in the late 1940s and early 1950s. For the first time surgeons were able to see the damaged heart they were operating on. In 1953 such an operation was performed at the University of Minnesota, Minneapolis, using hypothermia. The surgery to correct a major defect was so hazardous that the patient could never have survived it had his body been at its normal temperature. His heart would have been unable to pump enough oxygenated blood to support life and to supply his brain during the operation.

So he was cooled until his body could manage on only half its normal quantity of oxygen.

That same year, thirteen successful open-heart operations were performed at the University of Colorado Medical Center in Denver. Doctors there also brought safety to the patients by using cold. Each patient was given a drug to keep him from shivering and was then placed in a tub filled with lukewarm water. The doctors had found the kind of tub they needed at the Colorado Psychiatric Hospital where deeply disturbed mental patients are given long baths to soothe them. Hypothermia in this case was to soothe the body's needs, rather than those of the mind. Ice cubes were gradually added to the water in the tub and stirred around the patient with a wooden paddle. It took only 8 to 12 minutes to bring down the temperature of a child to between 86° and 89.6°F. Small adults required about half an hour and large ones a whole hour. Once the desired temperature was reached, the patient was rushed to the operating table.

The combination of hypothermia and this new kind of surgery proved to be a winning one and surgeons began to correct defects that would formerly have been crippling or fatal. Babies born with heart abnormalities were operated on, sometimes when they were no more than a few weeks old. Children who had never been able to play with friends or to go to school were made healthy. Several pregnant women with heart defects underwent surgery and later gave birth to normal babies. Men and women who had been barely clinging to life for years were able to work again and lead active lives.

COLD AGAINST DISEASE

Hypothermia alone had provided quite enough protection in the early days of open-heart surgery, but as the operations became longer and more complicated, the heart and lungs needed to be relieved of all activities.

A way of doing this was conceived by a young research fellow at Harvard University in 1931, years before open-heart surgery was performed, and even before Dr. Fay brought hypothermia into modern medicine. At three o'clock on an afternoon of that year a woman developed an obstruction in her lung and was rushed into surgery. Dr. John H. Gibbon, Jr., was present at the operation, and sat with the patient all night long watching life slowly ebb from her body. As the hours passed Dr. Gibbon began to speculate on whether she might have been saved had it been possible to remove the blood from her body, put oxygen in and take carbon dioxide out of it, and then to return the oxygenated blood to her circulatory system. Both heart and lungs would be bypassed while the surgery was performed. There was, of course, no way achieving that then, and at a few minutes after eight o'clock in the morning, the woman died.

Dr. Gibbon went to other assignments, but could not get the idea out of his mind. At last he decided to try to develop a machine himself with the aid of his young wife. And the day came when the two placed a cat on the crude device they had built and watched it take over all the work of heart and lungs. The animal was kept on the machine for 39 minutes, and survived. They soon found that drastic as the method seemed, it brought no ill effects. One cat had a litter of nine healthy kittens only 2 months after the device was tested on her.

The machine was further improved and successful experiments on dogs were performed. All of this took years; Dr. Gibbon did not feel ready to use his machine on a human patient until 1953. At that time he learned of an 18-year-old girl with a heart defect so serious that a very long operation was needed. The heart-lung machine was brought into the operating room. For 26 minutes the machine circulated oxygenated blood through the girl's body while the defect was being repaired. Then her own heart and lungs were able to take over. The girl recovered, and the machine became part of standard hospital equipment.

If heart and brain operations are safer when the patient is cooled nine or twelve degrees below normal, what would happen if he were really cold, if his body temperature were forced to fall twenty, thirty, thirty-five, or even more degrees below its customary level? Longer and even more complicated operations could then be performed.

The icy tub or cooling blanket could not possibly bring about such drastic results. Really low temperature can only be obtained in a way that sounds impossible: The body must be chilled from the inside out, rather than from the outside in. The heart, liver, lungs, and kidneys get cold before the skin does. As these are in the core of the body, this is known as core cooling. Internal chilling is brought about by the circulation of cold blood through the system. Warm blood is drawn from vein or artery and forced through a heat exchanger. This is a simple refrigerating device using ice water as the coolant. Once the blood's warmth is removed, it is returned to the circulation. The heat exchanger is frequently attached to the heart-lung machine that is supporting the patient during the whole process.

It is also possible to cool the body from the inside without opening the chest at all. As might be expected, this is most often done when the surgery is to be performed on another part of the body. Blood in such cases may come from the main artery of a thigh. It is pumped from there through a heat exchanger and an oxygenator before being put back into the artery on the other thigh. The cooled blood can bring the body temperature to 59°F in about half an hour.

And what happens to the system then? By the time the temperature has reached 68°F the blood flow is down to 10 to 15 percent of its former speed. At 59°F the metabolism just about grinds to a halt. The heart stops beating and no longer sends oxygenated blood to the brain. But the brain can take it. At that low temperature the organ can remain without oxygen or blood for half an hour or more without harm to its thinking powers.

The kidney and liver, along with the brain and heart, are particularly bloody organs. When cold slows the heavy flow of blood, operations on these organs are both easier for the surgeon to perform and less risky for the patient.

Should the body be chilled to 82.4°F the circulation to the kidney can be broken off for an hour and if the temperature is dropped to between 77° and 68°F, the period can be extended to 2 hours.

While accepting the good that is done by hypothermia, one must not overlook some unfortunate side effects and aftereffects. For example,

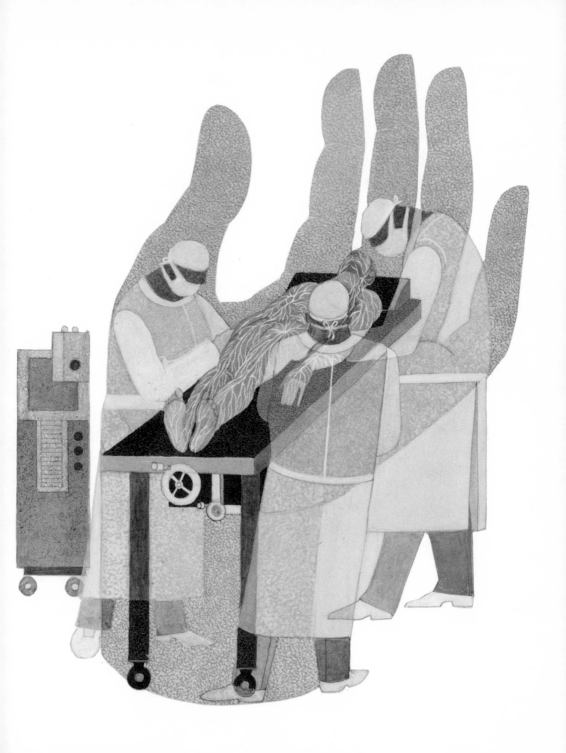

when the kidney operation is over, and the patient is rewarmed, his kidney may not begin to function properly for an entire day and night.

The effect of cold on the heart can be more significant. If the body is cooled to far below normal, certain muscle fibers in the heart may begin to quiver independently and without rhythm. Three-quarters of a group of patients cooled for surgery at Duke University Medical Center, Durham, North Carolina, developed this condition. Although there are ways of treating the quivering, it still presents a danger.

Some of the problems associated with modern hypothermia were recognized centuries ago. At that time they were observed as the result of exposure to the natural cold of winter. In 1683 Robert Boyle, an English scientist and philosopher, described the effect of cold on knights in armor in gruesome fashion: "Cold seizes men's Bodies in the reins and all about the Wast (and especially horse-men underneath the Armor of the Back and Breast) and straightens those parts so forcibly that it freezes all the parts of the Belly, especially the Guts." He described this as a "gangrene of the Guts," and added the unpleasant detail that it prevented "descent of Excrements downwards."

Today the scientific basis for the suffering of these knights is understood. Intestinal activity drops markedly as body temperature falls. In fact, when a person is chilled to 86°, all gastric function stops. As a result, stomach upsets are the most common aftereffects of even mild hypothermia.

On the other hand, just to make the situation thoroughly confusing, cooling can also relieve gastric distress. In 1894 a French chemist,

Raoul Pictet, was suffering torments from constant stomach pains. The prescriptions given him by doctors had brought him no relief. One day he decided to sit down in what he called a "cold well" for 15 minutes. That night, he later announced gleefully, he ate a full dinner for the first time in many years. From then on he recommended "frigotherapy" to anyone with digestive difficulties.

Some modern physicians believe that cooling—brought about in a hospital rather than in Pictet's "cold well"—can help to relieve ulcers.

The possibility that chilling of the body might control cancer was first suggested in the 1930s. This was some years before the attempts to kill cancers by means of cryosurgery. Although both cryosurgery and hypothermia have to do with cold, they are really quite different. Cryosurgery involves the limited use of temperature so fantastically low that it totally and rapidly destroys a given group of cells. Hypothermia, on the other hand, is a much more moderate cold. It effects its changes in more subtle ways. The idea that hypothermia could help cancer victims seems reasonable. Cancers are seldom found on the hands and feet, and these are colder than the rest of the body. Cooling the entire body to about 86°F then might keep a cancer elsewhere in the body from growing. This attractive theory, however, has not worked out. Even when patients were chilled with core cooling to temperatures lower than that, their cancers did not improve.

A newer theory, now being tested experimentally, suggests that a cancer might be destroyed if it were kept warm while the rest of the body were cooled. Dr. Vojin Popovic of Emory University Medical

School in Atlanta, Georgia, has tried this out on male hamsters with cancers of the cheek pouch. After being lightly anesthetized, the animals were placed in a cold-water bath where body temperatures fell to 39.2°F. Unlike the human, the hamster reaches such temperatures with relative ease and speed. A little heating coil around the tumor kept it at 98.6°F, a normal thermometer reading for human and hamster alike. At the end of 2 hours some of the hamsters were lifted out of the bath and rewarmed. The tumors continued to grow. Clearly, 2 hours had not been enough time. A second group was given 4 hours in the bath. The tumors shrank, but in 5 or 6 days they grew back. The last of the hamsters were chilled for 10 hours. The cancers shrank rapidly and within 15 days all were completely gone. What is more, not one tumor grew back. Even more startling was the finding that only the cancer cells had died; the cheek pouch tissue around them soon returned to normal.

Why did it happen? No one is quite sure. Dr. Popovic suggests that the metabolism of cancer cells may be higher than that of normal tissues. When the cells near the cancer are cool their metabolism is slowed. They may then no longer be able to provide the warm tumor cells with the amount of oxygen and nutrients needed for growth. Body circulation is slower, too, so the cancer cells may be unable to get rid of their waste products.

Heating the tumor, cooling the body, and then giving a powerful anticancer drug in a triple-pronged attack on cancer is also being tested by Dr. Popovic and a number of other researchers. The drug, 5-

fluorouracil, has been known for a long time, but its use was limited because it is so strong that it may kill some healthy tissues along with the cancerous ones. Yet if a patient is under hypothermia, he can more easily stand this and other anticancer drugs. When 5-fluorouracil was given to cooled dogs with warm tumors, the cancer cells died.

Doctors warn, though, that the effectiveness of cooling for controlling cancer will not be proved for years—if, indeed, it ever is.

Whatever the ultimate results with cancer, hypothermia is already accepted as a valuable medical tool. New uses for low body temperature are being found every year. Chilling is helpful for such different conditions as bleeding after childbirth, emphysema (a lung disease), cirrhosis of the liver, relief of pain, and heat stroke. Severely burned animals have been helped by cooling; the same could well be true for humans.

Open-heart surgery remains the major use for hypothermia today. The development of this technique has had far-reaching effects. Several years ago an open-heart operation was performed at the University of Minnesota by Dr. John F. Lewis. He was one of the first surgeons to recognize the importance of hypothermia for such surgery. Among his associates at the university that year was a young South African doctor, named Christiaan Neethling Barnard.

9. ONE DECEMBER DAY IN CAPETOWN

What was the most startling medical event of the 1960s? The answer most frequently given to that question describes an operation that was performed on the third of December, 1967, in Capetown, South Africa. On that day a human heart was taken from a dead body and transplanted into a living person.

A great deal was written about the skill and daring of the surgeon, Dr. Christiaan Barnard. "It was like watching a bullfight. Certain classical maneuvers had to be done before the grand finale," said one of his fellow doctors. But in all the reports of the operation, little was told of the important part that was played by cold.

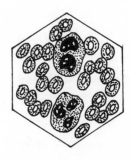

Louis Washkansky, a wholesale grocer, married and the father of a 14-year-old boy, had entered Groote Schuur Hospital earlier in the fall, dying of a badly damaged heart. Dr. Barnard, who had been transplanting many hearts in animals, came to Washkansky's bedside and made his revolutionary suggestion.

"I was petrified," Washkansky's wife, Ann, said later, "but my husband had such confidence in medical men that he inspired me as well."

Thus, the Washkanskys began the nerve-racking wait for a suitable donor to appear. On the first Saturday in December pretty, dark-haired 25-year-old Denise Ann Darvall went out to buy a cake. While running across the street to the bakery, she was struck by a car. Close to death, she was rushed to the emergency room at Groote Schuur Hospital. Severe though her injuries were, the heart was untouched. Dr. Barnard was called and he decided it was the moment to act. He rushed to Denise's father and asked for the gift of her heart. The request was granted less than an hour before Denise's death.

The immediate problem faced by Dr. Barnard was that of keeping the dead heart from spoiling before it could be placed in Washkansky's chest. Although a dead body will become cold in the natural course of events, the internal organs undergo harmful changes before then. Denise's body, therefore, was quickly chilled to 78.8°F and her heart to 60.8°F. Working with considerable speed, Dr. Barnard had the heart out of the body in 2 minutes and placed it in a bowl containing a cold solution which further reduced the temperature to 50°F.

While all these actions were being completed, Washkansky was put under anesthesia in a second operating room. A heart-lung machine was attached to his body to circulate blood when he was between hearts. The moment was approaching when Washkansky would have to endure the exceedingly dangerous operation. Dr. Barnard then turned to cold, knowing that the very changes in metabolism brought about by a low body temperature transform a risky operation into one that is considerably safer. Washkansky's temperature was dropped to 76°F, to 71.6°F, and finally to a low point of 70.88°F. The need for oxygen fell and his blood flow slowed markedly.

The heart was then removed from his cold body and the strong young heart of Denise Darvall was carefully put into the empty space and sewn in place. The new heart was in the body, but the question still remained: Would it beat again? Could it pump blood through the veins of a middle-aged male body so different from that of the young woman to whom it had so recently belonged? A single electric shock was given to stimulate the heart. It stirred in response and began to beat faster and faster, reaching a rate of 120 beats per minute. "It's going to work!" exclaimed Dr. Barnard triumphantly. The heart-lung machine was removed, leaving the transplanted heart to take over the full task of circulation. Washkansky's body had been gradually re-warmed and was making normal demands for blood and oxygen.

Within a day, news of what had happened in Capetown appeared on the front pages of newspapers all over the world. To many, the replacement of a heart seemed to be little less than a miracle. No other part of the body has been the subject of so much poetry, story and song. The heart is the seat of emotion. We feel with it, love with it. And it is shattered not by clogged arteries or damaged valves, but by a loss of love—or so the poets tell us. But, of course, whatever the poetic imagery, the heart is just a pump and can, therefore, go from body to body as it did from Denise Darvall to Washkansky.

Millions of people began to follow Washkansky's fight for life. He soon felt strong enough for a television interview and joked: "I'm a Frankenstein now. I've got somebody else's heart." He had obviously failed to read the novel of that name or to see the old horror movie; otherwise he would have known that Frankenstein was the doctor, not the monster. The important point, to be sure, is not whether he was right, but that he was healthy enough to joke.

117

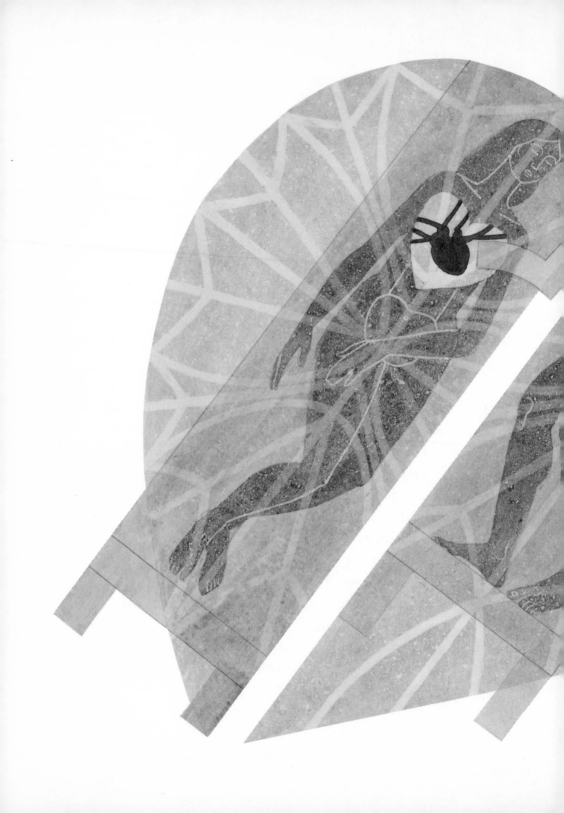

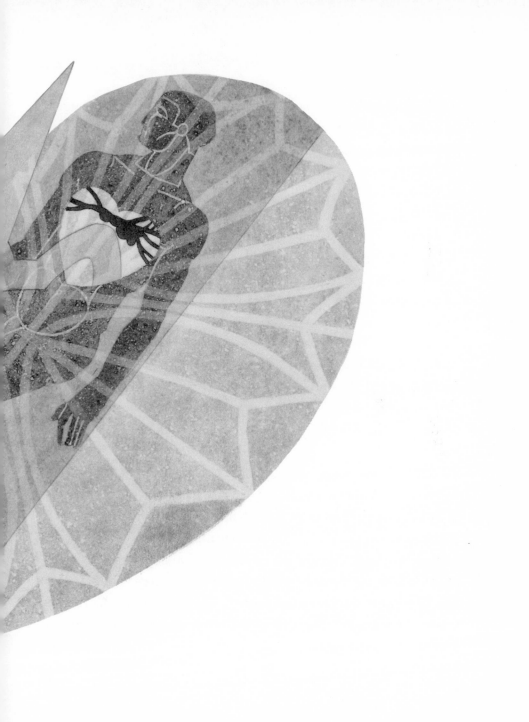

COLD AGAINST DISEASE

Everything seemed to be going well, and then 13 days after surgery, Washkansky caught pneumonia. On the twenty-first of December, he died. He had, nonetheless, survived long enough to prove that a transplanted heart was capable of supporting life. It was, after all, the infection that killed him; the heart, like any other, failed only at the end.

At the time of Washkansky's death, the public was belatedly learning that the medical profession had been expecting a successful transplant. Research into transplantation had been going on all over the world for some years. By 1967, although very few people outside of research centers knew about it, a scientific race was on. Heart surgeons in hospitals separated by thousands of miles were ready to perform a transplant and were hoping desperately for an opportunity. No one really expected Dr. Barnard to win this race. Most insiders had been betting on Dr. Norman E. Shumway of Stanford University School of Medicine, Palo Alto, California, who had developed the transplantation technique that was to be used by many others, including Dr. Barnard. He was not, however, even to be the runner up. Dr. Barnard beat his closest competitor, Dr. Adrian Kantrowitz, then at Maimonides Hospital Medical Center in Brooklyn, New York, only by days. Dr. Kantrowitz felt the loss keenly, commenting: "That's why I'm not a hero in Brooklyn." He and his medical team at Maimonides had prepared for the anticipated event by operating on more than 250 dogs. One of them, a puppy named Eterna, was cooled to 60.8°F for the transplant operation. She was up and walking around and drinking water by the following day. Eterna went on to live like any normal dog during the 7 months she survived with her new heart.

Dr. Kantrowitz, like Dr. Barnard, had spent the last days of November waiting for a suitable donor to turn up. His patient was not a middle-aged man, but rather a newborn baby with a defective heart. This made the search more difficult; only another newborn could have a heart small enough to be of use. And it had to be an infant dead or dying of a condition that did not affect the heart. Dr. Kantrowitz sent telegrams to 500 hospitals asking that he be informed the moment an infant was born with a sound heart and hopelessly damaged brain. While he was waiting, Dr. Barnard performed his historic operation in South Africa.

Two days later, a baby with a severe brain defect was born. He lived a mere 2 days. The parents, saying that they hoped someone else would have joy out of their sorrow, had already agreed to let the heart be taken. The donor baby, like Denise Darvall, was chilled to protect the heart from damage. The infant who was to receive the new heart was cooled to 62.6°F and the operation got underway. After the transplanted heart had been put in place, it started easily with just one shock, as Washkansky's new heart had done. It continued to beat steadily while the baby's temperature was returned to normal. Then 5 hours after the operation, the infant began to sink and in another $1\frac{1}{2}$ hours, he was dead. The cause of death, Dr. Kantrowitz believes, was hypothermia. Lowering the body temperature of an infant carries some risk of disastrous side effects. The normal balance of the body may be thrown too far off. The method of cooling which has saved so many during surgery did not help the baby here.

COLD AGAINST DISEASE

The failure of the second transplant did not bring this form of surgery to a halt. It was used, after all, only on patients so close to death that any step, however drastic, seemed worth the risk. The dramatic operation was performed in hospitals in many cities of the world. A French priest, Father Boulogne, who had been bedridden for a year was given the heart of a man dead of a brain hemorrhage. During the operation the donor's body was cooled to 86°F and his heart to 68°F. Within a few months, Father Boulogne had returned to his parishioners and was able to lead a fairly normal life for the $1\frac{1}{2}$ years he survived. The heart of a young sailor was donated to a man of 60 in Sydney, Australia. The first Russian transplant took place 11 months after Dr. Barnard's success. The patient, a Leningrad woman of 25, lived for only 33 hours.

Of all heart transplant operation survivors, none received more attention than Dr. Barnard's second such patient, Dr. Philip Blaiberg, a retired dentist aged 58. Almost every move he made during the $19\frac{1}{2}$ months of his life with his new heart was photographed and commented on in the press. Although he insisted to the end that his prolonged life had been satisfactory enough to make up for all the pain and worry, his wife said he had been uncomfortable and ill. Dr. Blaiberg's survival record was soon to be broken by Louis B. Russell, Jr., a junior high school teacher in Indianapolis, Indiana. He was given the heart of a teen-ager in an operation performed at the Medical College of Virginia in Richmond, by Dr. Richard Lower, who had worked with Dr. Norman Shumway to devise the classic transplant method. Russell enjoyed far better health than Dr. Blaiberg had.

He returned to his job and had enough energy left over to repair the roof of his house and to make furniture. Nonetheless, neither Dr. Lower nor Russell received as much praise and world-wide publicity as had been lavished on Dr. Barnard and Dr. Blaiberg.

Although receiving the lion's share of attention, Dr. Barnard has not performed the largest number of transplants. The record-holder for the first year was handsome, youthful Dr. Denton A. Cooley who was then on the staff of St. Luke's Episcopal Hospital in Houston, Texas. At a medical conference held in 1968, Cooley called to the platform an example of his medical skill—a 54-year-old man in whose chest was beating the heart of a 17-year-old boy.

Dr. Cooley is able to perform a transplant operation in an incredible 2 hours. The actual substitution of the heart is done in 30 minutes or less. Working at such speed, he has been able to give up body cooling. Other transplant surgeons, however, have continued to use it.

In the 2 years following the surgery on Washkansky, 150 heart transplants were performed on 148 patients (two received a second heart when the first failed). Twenty survived for longer than a year— much of the time in relatively good health.

What kills a person whose new heart is able to pump blood effectively? There are two main causes of death, and although they sound different, they are in truth related: infection and rejection.

As has been observed in the lesser transplant of skin, the body refuses to accept foreign cells whether they be harmful bacteria or helpful organs. While the mechanism of rejection, known as the immune reaction, is complex, it depends greatly on the action of certain white blood cells or lymphocytes. No way has yet been found of preventing the reaction altogether, but it can be delayed. Certain drugs and radiation destroy the lymphocytes and foil the immune reaction. But this is where the infection problem crops up. Tampering with the rejection system makes the body lose its ability to recognize and react to viral or bacterial invaders. Consequently, the transplant recipient all too often dies of a disease that seems to have no connection with his new organ. Washkansky, to take the best known case, died of pneumonia.

In any case, rejection is less likely to happen and occurs more slowly when the foreign cells are similar to those of the person receiving them. Identical twins, alone among mankind, can pass tissues from one to the other without triggering the immune reaction. There are relatively few occasions, though, when a twin can be used as a donor. Fortunately, surprising as it seems, some strangers are related to one another in the composition of tissues. When someone needs a transplant, a large number of tests is performed on his cells and those of all possible donors. In this way the suitable stranger is found among them. The closer the tissue match, the greater is the chance of a successful transplant.

The match is graded like schoolwork, from A to F. A matches occur only between identical twins and B matches are rather rare. Surgeons will seldom agree to perform a transplant on patients when the match is poorer than C, and many consider that to be unpromising. Enough differences remain even between the B matches, however, to require some drug or x-ray treatment. Tests show that Dr. Blaiberg was exceptionally well matched with his donor, and yet he needed drugs to keep him from rejecting the new heart right away.

Research into better ways of avoiding rejection is continuing and many surgeons and laboratory workers believe the problem will in time be solved.

There are hints that freezing may affect the rejection process for certain tissues. Transplants of bone marrow, for example, have succeeded in the past only when the marrow was given by a twin, or more rarely a brother or sister. Animal experiments, however, indicate that frozen bone marrow is not rejected as rapidly as fresh. Mice with marrow severely damaged by x-rays recovered when they were given injections of frozen guinea pig bone marrow. It is too early to say whether people will respond in a similar manner and accept the cells of an unrelated donor.

Of all organs being transplanted today, the rejection problem is least acute for the kidney. If that organ fails, the patient can be kept alive on an artificial kidney machine until another donor appears. In addition, as each person has two kidneys, it is possible to find a donor among the living as well as the dead. This greatly increases the chances of getting tissue matches in the top grades. In fact, the first successful organ transplant was of a kidney taken from one identical twin and given to the other. That operation was performed in 1954, 13 years before Dr. Barnard and his triumph. A relative is also a good donor and many brothers, sisters, fathers and mothers have given up a kidney to keep someone they love alive.

Most other organs, to be sure, must be taken from the dead. One donor could contribute organs to as many as seventeen people, Dr. C.

COLD AGAINST DISEASE

Walton Lillehei, chief of surgery at New York Hospital in New York City, points out, provided that so many good tissue matches could be made. Whatever the organ, the chance of successful transplantation is improved when the patient is cooled. Transplants have been made of such parts of the anatomy as the liver, lungs, pancreas, adrenal glands, gastrointestinal tract, spleen, thymus, and larynx.

And what of the brain? It would seem logical for the brain to be the most sensitive of all organs and the quickest to reject foreign matter. Instead it accepts grafts of tissue more easily than other organs do.

The feat of transplanting the entire brain has been challenging scientists for many years. In the early 1960s Dr. Vladimir P. Demikhov of the USSR implanted a puppy's entire head and upper body in the neck of a big dog. For 29 days, Demikhov reported, the transposed head could bite, swallow, and react to pain. While this was a step in the right direction, it was obviously of no benefit either to puppy or large dog.

A team of doctors at Western Reserve University Medical School, Cleveland, Ohio, headed by Dr. Robert J. White, professor of neurosurgery, then set out to transplant the brain alone. First they carefully removed the brains of six dogs. Each brain was placed in the neck of another dog and connected to his blood stream. The blood flow was stopped for 5 minutes during the transplantation. The brain was protected during this period by slightly lowered temperature. Then within the body of one stranger, the brain of another stranger was returned to life. Some dogs lived a few hours, others for as long as 2 days. How do we know they were alive? Brainwaves were recorded on an electro-encephalograph machine. The machine could not tell whether the brains were actually thinking and giving directions to the bodies that housed them.

Is the next step the actual transplantation of the brain? The idea seems like something out of a horror movie. One can imagine the college professor forgetting history and economics and the manual laborer suddenly able to do advanced mathematics and read Greek. But is it really that absurd? Consider the young man doomed by a deep-seated brain tumor, or the elderly woman slipping into a second childhood due to hardening of the arteries of the brain. Might not their only hope for a useful life be the gift of another brain or part of a brain?

The great future of brain transplantation, though, must lie not in restoring mental health to adult or aged, but in giving it to the unborn or newborn. Each year many infants are conceived who have no chance of a normal life, if indeed they have any life at all. Some defects can already be diagnosed before birth. Babies enter the world with hardly a brain or with one so damaged that it will never work properly. Perhaps the normal brain of an unborn infant dead of some unrelated cause might be removed, preserved briefly by means of chilling, and then implanted into the defective embryo. The brain of an infant dead at birth might be given to an otherwise damaged newborn.

Should brain transplantation be perfected—and this may happen before too many years have passed—a once doomed baby would come into the world capable of leading a normal, happy life.

10. TOO FEW HEARTS

"Drive carefully; Dr. Barnard is waiting," goes the slogan on a button worn by teen-agers.

A bum in a cartoon is lying on a park bench. The caption reads, "Just resting, not a heart donor."

The shortage of donors grows steadily more acute and has become a major transplantation stumbling block.

Some surgeons are looking to nonhuman sources. The transplantation era began in this way. The very first heart transplant ever performed on a human being received very little attention. Yet it took place several years before Dr. Barnard operated on Washkansky. In

January of 1964 the heart of a large chimpanzee was implanted in the body of a man by Dr. James Hardy at the University of Mississippi Medical Center, in Jackson. The monkey heart managed to keep the human alive for about 1½ hours.

Several years afterward, transplant surgeon Dr. Denton Cooley was unable to locate a human heart donor for a desperately sick patient. He followed Dr. Hardy's example and tried an animal. In this case, the heart of a 125-pound sheep was placed in the dying man's chest. It was rejected almost immediately.

A reverse twist on this surgery was attempted at the Medical College of Virginia where the heart of an automobile-accident victim was transplanted into a baboon. The human heart was quickly rejected and the animal died.

When 47-year-old Haskell Karp was close to death and no donor appeared, Dr. Cooley tried a completely different approach. He implanted a completely artificial heart. This kept Karp alive for only 65 hours.

Most people today find the idea of plastic organs unnatural. The use of animal organs appears actually repulsive to others. Such alternative sources are being considered or tried, because the difficulty of finding enough human donors is so great.

When a good donor is found, he rapidly may be stripped of his organs. One evening in late August of 1968, Nelva Lou Hernandez had a violent quarrel with her husband. She seized a pistol that had been carelessly left lying around and screamed, "I'm going to shoot myself." She suited the action to the words, and after death her heart, both kidneys, and one lobe of a lung were removed. Each of four men then received the organ he needed. A few days later a public official in Sao Paulo, Brazil, shot himself to death. His heart went to the father of five children; his kidneys and pancreas to three other invalids.

Sometimes when a donor is found, efforts to make use of him are foiled. A strange occurrence put off a heart transplant operation scheduled at Stanford University Hospital, Palo Alto, California, in late October of 1968. The patient had been in the hospital for some time waiting for a donor. At last one night an 18-year-old youth was brought in with a gunshot wound. It looked like a typical suicide, and the boy died during the night. His heart was in perfect condition, but before the surgeons could get to work, the police telephoned. Another young man had been booked on suspicion of the murder and the would-be donor's body had to be examined more carefully. By the time it was finally released by the police, the heart was no longer in condition to be used for a transplant.

Even when murder is not involved, all too many desperately needed organs are wasted. They deteriorate before a transplant can be arranged. When the organ is chilled the harmful changes occur more slowly. Thus the period of time between removal of the organ from the donor and its safe use as a transplant can be extended somewhat.

"The impressive thing to me is the extreme temperature dependence of the cadaver organ," Dr. William Angell of Stanford University School of Medicine stated at a recent conference on transplantation.

The heart, therefore, is placed in a cold salt solution at about 50°F the moment after it is taken from the donor's body.

The liver kept at room temperature will become useless for a transplant in a mere 20 to 30 minutes. When chilled, the safety period stretches to at least 8 hours. While surgeons have been holding back from using livers stored longer than that for humans, animals have received transplants kept for much longer periods. Five dogs were given livers that had been held at 39°F for 24 hours; three of them sur-

vived. Also there have been cases in which livers have functioned after
5 days of cold storage.

In another experiment dogs got transplants of pancreas that had
been cooled to 39°F for 20 to 24 hours. Five of them recovered, one
living for 169 days.

Human kidney transplants have been made successfully with organs
chilled for 24 hours. A man in a remote rural area needed a kidney
transplant, and there was no possible donor within reach. His doctor
telegraphed medical centers where transplants were being made and a
donor was found in a city 2600 miles away. After removal, the
kidney was cooled and then flown the entire distance in a refrigerated
container. A transplant surgeon accompanied the organ, and the substitution was done.

Dog brains have been cooled to nearly 32°F. All activity naturally
came to a halt. After a period of 6 hours, some of the brains were rewarmed and the blood circulated again. They began to function. Other
brains held at this low temperature for as long as a month were also
restored to life upon rewarming. They were incapable of functioning
on a high level, however, and could not have been used as transplants.

If organs are to be stored for long, they must be frozen, not merely
chilled. While it might seem as feasible to freeze organs as to freeze
blood or sperm, this is not the case. Each organ is made up of many
different kinds of cells, and the freezing method that works for one
may destroy another.

The many failures in preserving organs by freezing, therefore, are not unexpected; what is surprising is that there should be any successes at all. Dr. Audrey Smith, known for her work with glycerol, froze the hearts of embryonic chickens in liquid nitrogen. When they were thawed, she could detect a normal heartbeat. No mammal heart has done as well.

"After twelve years of effort we have at last succeeded in freezing and thawing kidneys," states Dr. Herndon Lehr, who has been working with four other physicans and an electrical engineer at the University of Pennsylvania, in Philadelphia. After thawing, the kidneys were then implanted into three dogs; in each case, the organ functioned.

"The thawing had been the stumbling block," adds Dr. Lehr, "because the kidneys were most damaged during that stage."

The injury was avoided when the engineer, Frederick D. Ketterer, turned to a microwave oven that heated the organs with greater speed than had been possible before.

This work has already led to the establishment of an experimental frozen organ bank. So far, in addition to the kidney, it holds the parathyroid and small bowel. All are treated with a protective substance, frozen, and then stored in liquid nitrogen.

It may yet take years to bring even so limited a frozen organ bank out of the experimental stage. And a bigger bank containing hearts, brains, and lungs lies even farther off in the scientific future. But many biologists believe the day will come when this will be in use. The sick person will then be able to go to the organ bank and withdraw the liver, pancreas, heart, or gastrointestinal tract deposited there months, possibly years before by somebody else. And he would not need to accept a substitute organ made of plastic or resort to the transplanted heart or lungs of a chimpanzee.

11. COLD BRAINS

In a laboratory in Cleveland a monkey's brain was suspended in a strange device. Nothing of the body that once housed it remained, except for two small bones to help support it. Yet this brain was alive. It may even have had thoughts, felt hunger or thirst, experienced sensations, been happy, angry, or afraid. No arteries and veins carried blood from heart to brain, but then, of course, there was no heart. Instead, plastic tubes circulated blood taken from another, larger monkey. In this way, far from the living organism that once had sheltered it, the brain lived on.

"I don't query the usefulness of keeping a monkey's brain alive for

18 hours while unconnected with the monkey's body, a feat just performed in Cleveland," wrote a humor magazine. "I only wonder what the brain was thinking about during that time."

But then, no one knows what a whole monkey thinks about either. The fact that it was still able to think at all—after being removed from the skull and body and attached to the device—is a tribute to cold. The brain was kept at temperatures ranging from 82.4° to 89.6°F during the transfer.

If the brain alone can be cooled successfully outside of the body, what of the brain inside it? And for that matter, what of the heart, kidneys, liver, or bladder? As use of hypothermia increased, surgeons began to ask whether it were indeed necessary to cool an entire body in order to operate on just a small part of it. That seemed an extremely roundabout and inefficient method. Then, too, it is sometimes desirable to avoid hypothermia. Not everyone can afford to risk the possible side or aftereffects. When the whole body is cooled to operate on the liver, for example, the kidney that is not really involved is affected. Stomach upsets can add to the general discomfort following surgery. In the course of a brain operation, the cold heart may begin to quiver.

In the mid-1960s, a 56-year-old man with a brain tumor entered a hospital for treatment. Hypothermia by then was recognized as a way of guarding the brain during difficult operations, but the surgeon believed that this man could not endure the stress of whole body cooling. And so the decision was made to cool only his brain. Its temperature was dropped to 53.2°F in the space of just 17 minutes, while the heart and other internal organs remained at 95°F or higher. Circulation of blood to the brain was stopped for slightly less than half an hour while the tumor was removed. The brain was then rewarmed and 2 hours later the patient regained consciousness.

A way of cooling the brain—and just the brain—had been sought for many years before that. In the beginning, surgeons bathed the brain surface with cold solutions or applied ice directly to the cerebral hemispheres. These methods did lower brain temperature, but they were extremely difficult to control. In addition, the area cooled was much too small. And so a system that is successful in chilling the entire body from the inside out was modified so as to apply to the brain alone.

Warm blood is taken from the main artery in the patient's thigh and pumped at a rate of slightly more than a quart a minute to a heat exchanger. There it is chilled to the desired temperature and forced up through a bubble trap. This catches not only bubbles, but also any impurities which might have gotten into the blood during its journey. Then with warmth removed, the blood is returned to the body at neck level. The amount of chilled blood entering the system is not great enough to cool the body below the neck. Once the brain is cool, the flow of blood can be stopped at the level of one of the vertebrae for the actual operation. The brain is then not only cold, but also bloodless.

Oddly enough, the first attempt to cool the brain in this way did not take place during a brain operation. In 1956, Japanese surgeons lowered brain temperature so as to reduce the risks of open-heart surgery. They showed that it was possible to stop the heart and thus the circulation of blood to the brain for 13 minutes without damaging the cooled brain. This record has since been broken many times. And in time, the method was applied to brain surgery as well.

Once the use of brain cooling in surgery was established, physicians began to consider other applications. Some have gone so far as to try it as a treatment for epilepsy, a nervous system disease in which the victim periodically has fits or convulsions. Most, but not all, epileptic patients are helped by drugs. Those who resist drug treatment have been candidates for cooling. One 16-year-old boy, for example, was having

several severe attacks every day, even though he was taking large doses of drugs. After his brain was cooled, he had no convulsions for a year. Although they recurred, it was possible to control them with reasonable amounts of drugs.

Local cooling of the brain had been done for several years before anyone thought of trying the same thing on the spinal cord. This is odd, because as Dr. Juan Negrin, Jr., attending neurosurgeon of Lenox Hill Hospital, in New York City, remarks, "It is reasonable to expect spinal cord and brain tissue to react similarly under low temperatures." And this is just what happens.

The technique of spinal cord cooling, however, is quite different from that of brain cooling. The cord itself is bathed with a cold solution. Minor surgery must be performed in order to insert tubes to carry the refrigerant.

Experiments were performed on dogs with rigid and convulsed muscles as a result of nervous system disorders. The muscles relaxed. The question remained whether the same procedure would work for people.

Dr. Negrin's first eight patients were victims of one form of cerebral palsy, a brain disease, and they ranged in age from 7 to 19. All were spastic and moved jerkily; they had stiff arms or legs that were hard to lift and bend. This changed after the spinal cord was cooled. One little girl, who had stumbled constantly even when supported by special crutches, was able to walk by herself. Another had been unable to control either hands or legs, but had clumsily groped around. She became able to feed herself and to use crutches effectively.

Multiple sclerosis is another nervous system disease often accompanied by jerky muscle movements and severe pain. Several patients have been relieved by spinal cord chilling.

But Dr. Negrin warns that neither cerebral palsy nor multiple sclerosis is cured by the chilling: "It is the symptom that is cured, not the disease."

The method has had its failures, too. Some patients, particularly those with multiple sclerosis, have suffered relapses.

During the time when spinal cord cooling was being performed on people with nervous system diseases, an elderly woman came to her doctor begging him to do something to relieve the never-ending pain caused by her severe arthritis. As a last resort, her spinal cord was bathed in the cold solution. After this, for the first time in years, the woman was able to sleep through the night without being awakened by the need for pain-killing drugs. The same treatment was later tried on a number of patients with painful cancers and they, too, were helped.

There is yet another kind of pain that has been impossible to relieve, because it does not really exist in the body. How is one to calm the agony of a wound that has healed, the ache of a tooth that has been removed? The leg has been taken off long ago, but the amputee complains that it still hurts. The agony may be the result of a chain of reflex activity that was set up within the spinal cord at the time of injury or amputation. Perhaps prolonged cooling of the cord might break that chain and end the pain forever.

Paralysis can be the real and tragic result of an injury to the spinal cord. In order to see whether cooling could help, Dr. Robert White of Western Reserve University Medical School, the man who isolated the monkey's brain, and a co-worker, Dr. Maurice Albin, went to work on 35 monkeys. First they caused an injury that would surely produce paralysis, and then they tried to undo the damage by bathing the spinal cord with a cold solution until its temperature fell to below 50°F. The rest of the body remained warm. A few days after the local cooling, all the monkeys were up and walking around. Should a person be injured in an accident, such success, says Dr. White, will depend on his getting to a hospital quickly. The spinal cord must be cooled within 6 hours of the injury. Swelling is then reduced and pressure on the spinal cord relieved before damage is done.

The system of cooling just one target area of the body is not limited to the central nervous system. Certain types of heart operations are performed on a cooled heart in a warm body. Similarly, the kidney, urinary bladder, and other internal organs may be chilled singly. Cooling in such cases may be brought about with pump and heat exchanger, as is done for the brain, or with cold applied directly, as is done for the spinal cord. The area may also be packed in slush or ice cubes.

After the large number of triumphs for regional cooling, doctors turned to the stomach. If slight chilling could relieve intestinal distress, as Pictet in the last century had observed, really low temperatures might help patients with ulcers. Perhaps, said Dr. Owen H. Wangensteen of the University of Minnesota Hospital, freezing the stomach wall would prevent the flow of ulcer-producing acid altogether. In order to bring this about, he had ulcer patients swallow a small rubber balloon. This came to rest in the stomach next to the ulcer. Then cold alcohol at temperatures ranging from $1.4°$ to $-4°F$ was circulated through the balloon. This treatment, said the first group, made them feel much better. Gradually the acid production increased again and the ulcers became troublesome. Dr. Wangensteen then froze the stomach wall again.

As reports of the success were published, large numbers of people with ulcers came to receive the freezing treatment. Many were disappointed. And in time a number of physicians at Dr. Wangensteen's own hospital turned against the technique and declared that freezing was no better than the old-fashioned, tried-and-true ways of treating ulcers with milk, a bland diet, and antacid pills.

But Dr. Wangensteen continues to defend his method. He points out that he has improved on his original technique and is now rapidly rewarming the stomach after freezing.

In any event, even if local hypothermia should be abandoned for ulcer patients, it will continue to be used as a treatment of other conditions. Cooling succeeds often enough to survive an occasional failure —if that should prove to be the case here.

As Dr. Negrin comments of the successes and failures of the type of regional cooling he performs: "When I get discouraged, I think of the people I have helped whom I could not have helped a few years ago. I have seen spastics who could not walk, walk; people who could not work, work; people in excruciating pain relieved."

12. SPACE, TIME, AND SPECIES

How long is the journey to another planet? A round trip to Mars, allowing 3 months for exploration, would take at least 2 years. And man is not likely to be satisfied for long with so limited a goal. Unmanned probes will go off to Jupiter and the colder planets more distant from earth's sun, and will be followed eventually by manned spacecraft. Platforms will be placed in orbit around the earth and in time serve as jumping-off places for ships setting off on long missions into the vastness of space.

As missions grow more ambitious, the possibilities of mishaps to the astronauts increase. A capsule could hurtle through space for

months or years until it at last drew close to the planet that was its destination. A team of astronauts would transfer to a small landing module and reach the surface. The men would get down and walk over the unfamiliar terrain, making observations and performing experiments. All at once, one of them could stumble, lose his footing and fall, hitting his head on a rock with such force that he could lose consciousness. His companion astronaut would help him back to the module and arrange for the return to the command ship. But what could be done for the wounded man once he arrived there? A medical kit would be available, and men trained in first aid, but the head injuries could be too severe to respond to such casual treatment. Perhaps the brain itself was damaged by the fall. On earth, as has been shown many times, cooling can protect the brain from swelling and bleeding. It would have the same effect in space.

Inducing hypothermia in outer space might seem to be every bit as difficult as performing brain surgery on the spot, but this is not the case. Certainly, it would not be possible to cool the brain alone with pump and heat exchanger, but lowering the temperature of the entire body moderately can be done. Special temperature controls on a space suit could make it function like the cooling blanket or mattress in a hospital. Any space medical kit would naturally include some anesthetic and tranquilizing drugs, and these could be used to control shivering.

The Russians are also considering this aspect of space medicine. They have tested an automatic device activated by remote control. Dogs have been chilled by it to 71.6° to 77°F and kept at that degree of cold for 5 days at a stretch.

Such a device might serve an explorer-astronaut who had shattered his leg in a fall from the ladder of the landing module. Or perhaps a meteorite could drop from above and strike a man with force. Whatever the injury, the victim can collapse and slip into shock. Lowering body temperature should work just as well in preventing shock in a spacecraft off Venus as on the battlefield.

A great deal of blood could be lost by an astronaut accident-victim, and no spacecraft can carry many pints for transfusions. The person's life might then depend on cold and its ability to reduce the body's need for circulating oxygenated blood.

The pain-killing qualities of chilling can mean as much to the men of space as it did to the ancient Greeks and Romans.

No matter how healthy the astronauts are when setting off, they could become ill in the course of a long voyage. A crew member might be infected by earthly germs that had slipped through the preflight sterilization procedure, possibly incubating in the body of a fellow astronaut. Cooling helps the system to withstand infection. Mountain snow provided by Saladin enabled Richard the Lion Hearted to fight off fever. In the days before the discovery of the wonder drugs, many sick people survived because they were cooled. Should supplies of antibiotics and other drugs run low when a spaceship was months away from earth, chilling could serve as at least a partial substitute.

While visiting another planet, an astronaut might be exposed to unearthly germs he had never met before and could not resist. Should he be made sick by a Martian germ, for example, hypothermia could keep him alive while biologists specializing in the study of unearthly life raced to discover its characteristics. Doctors would go on to determine the proper course of treatment. Once this had been decided upon, the victim of a space germ would be rewarmed and awakened from his cooled sleep.

On earth, the patient recovering from hypothermia can count on a gradual period of convalescence and care before he resumes his work and responsibilities. The astronaut, who is likely to be one of a three-

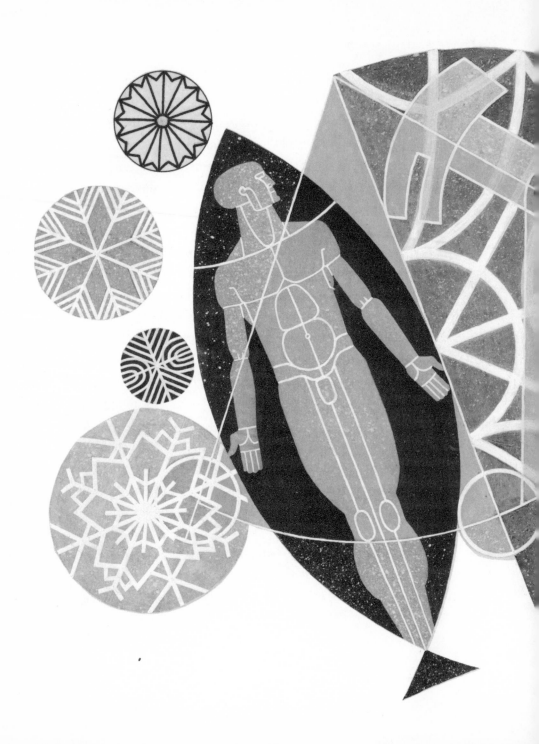

man team, must get back on the job as rapidly as possible and function at a high peak of efficiency. He has to perform the bewildering number of experiments and tasks he was taught during his training period. Those planning space missions, therefore, ask whether forcing the body to abandon its normal temperature range would bring about changes however slight in the ability to reason and remember.

In order to find this out, Dr. Vojin Popovic of Emory University cooled a group of rats to 84.2°F. Then they were sent to find food at the end of a confusing network of passages. The rats ran about the maze stupidly and sluggishly, bumping into each other, and retracing their steps constantly. The smell of the cheese did not stimulate them to greater effort.

"I then realized that a cold rat does not care about food," says Dr. Popovic. "I had to find something that would interest him. What would that be? Heat."

And so after chilling the rats, he returned them to their cages. A little heat lamp had been placed within. When a rat pressed a tiny lever with his paw, the lamp would be activated to send out a 2-second burst of heat. It took just 45 seconds for the chilled rats to catch on to the secret of the lever.

Such experiments and a study of the thousands of men, women, and children who have been chilled and later returned to normal mental health can be accepted as proof that intelligence is not lost. But what of memory, which is a most fragile part of man's intellectual capacity? Old people are likely to become forgetful before they lose their reasoning powers. And so it would be logical to assume that memory would most likely be affected by chilling.

Dr. Popovic, therefore, first trained rats to find food at the end of a maze. Then the rats were cooled. After some time had passed, they were rewarmed and led back to the maze. Without a moment's hesitation, the rodents ran through the passages and reached the cheese. It was as if the period spent at low temperature had never happened at all.

Many people believe that age takes a holiday in space. This is quite untrue. Aging occurs, because of changes in the heart and lungs and all the other organs and cells that make up the body. On the spacecraft as on earth, each breath and heartbeat carries the astronaut one bit nearer the grave.

But what happens if he undergoes hypothermia? The dimensions of time are then changed. Body functions are measured by time. The heart beats so many times a minute; the lungs take in so much air; the digestive processes advance just so far. Standards for these measurements are set at normal temperature. But the heart of the cooled astronaut or earthling beats more slowly; he inhales and exhales fewer times in a minute, and digests his food more slowly. What then can time mean to him? Does he gain a few days or hours of life?

Hypothermia can change not only the time dimension for man, it can even free him from the limitations of his own species.

Not even 25 years ago scientists were agreed that a warm-blooded, earthly animal could not exist for longer than a moment or two at a body temperature lower than 59°F. Then, in 1955, a frail woman with an incurable cancer, wishing to make her life count for something, offered herself as the subject of an experiment: She would be cooled to a temperature lower than any other human had ever survived. Cooling began and her temperature dropped lower and lower passing the "final" 59°F point and moving on down. Finally the thermometer registered 48.2°F. By this time her heart had stopped and she was no longer breathing. She lay like a dead woman for 45 minutes. Then the rewarming was started. For the first few moments there was no change; 15 minutes later the still heart aroused and began to beat again. She regained consciousness 10 hours after her temperature had returned to normal. "How cold was I?" was the first question she asked.

Doctors were stunned by the report of this case, yet within a very few years the record set by this woman was to be broken.

Surgeons at Duke University Medical Center were performing an extremely hazardous brain operation on a 39-year-old patient. His temperature was dropped degree by degree until it reached 39.56°F.

This is a fairly common winter temperature for a cold-blooded animal, such as a fish or snake. The seemingly impossible had happened: A warm-blooded human being had for a short time been transformed into a cold-blooded creature.

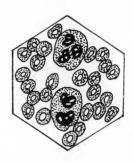

INDEX

INDEX

INDEX

ABOUT THE AUTHOR

Lucy Kavaler has been investigating the phenomena of cold for a number of years. In 1970 her major adult book on the subject, entitled *Freezing Point,* was published.

Cold Against Disease is the first of several books about "the wonders of cold" which the author intends to write.

Mrs. Kavaler is the author of the popular *Mushrooms, Molds, and Miracles.* She has written four other books on scientific subjects of interest to young people: *The Wonders of Fungi, The Wonders of Algae, The Artificial World Around Us,* and *Dangerous Air.*